11/13/75

MOVIN' OUT

**Equipment and Techniques
For Eastern Hikers**

by HARRY ROBERTS

**Stone Wall Press
Lexington, Massachusetts**

First printing

Library of Congress Card Number 74-25874
ISBN 0-913276-16-2

CONTENTS

1891323

For MOLLY, who knows why,

and for DICK KRAMER

who may never know why, but what else can you expect

from a guy who paddles an aluminum canoe?

ACKNOWLEDGMENTS

The publisher would like to thank all the kind folks at Eastern Mountain Sports in Boston for their invaluable editorial assistance with this book. Thanks also to Trak, Inc. for looking at the manuscript. Special thanks from the author to Trail North, Latham, N.Y., for their technical information and moral support.

PUBLISHER'S DISCLAIMER

Cartoons and Cover by Brian Penry.

Technical Illustrations by the author.

1. THE FIRST FEW STEPS

*"Willie, he tells me that doers and thinkers
Say movin's the closest thing to bein' free"*
— Billy Joe Shaver

I'm not here to pull your coat about the glories and wonders of hiking and back-packing. The fact that you're reading this book indicates that you're already inter-ested. Let's assume, though, that you've never really been on a trail. Maybe twenty years ago with the Scouts — once. Maybe for a lighthearted few hours down an abandoned tote road with a very special person. Maybe never. You'd like to begin, but there's a powerful lot of green out there, and too many people have given you too much conflicting advice about what it's like, and you're confused.

Well, if you sit on your butt all your life and never move out, you'll live and die confused — if you call that living. Let's move out. This Saturday or Sunday, if the weather is good. Go to your telephone book and look in the Yellow Pages under Camping Equipment and find a store that advertises backpacking and mountaineer-ing gear. Call them, and ask if they could recommend an easy trail nearby. If the store you called says "Huh?" or "Forget that, Charley! Wanna buy a Winnebago cheap?" hang up and call the next one. Sooner or later, you'll get a coherent, help-ful answer. Keep this shop in mind, by the way, if you decide that you like truck-ing around in the boonies. They're probably good folks to go to for equipment.

But right now, you could care less about equipment. You're going to mosey around a semi-civilized area for a few hours on Saturday, some place like a Nature Conservancy area or a state reforestation area or game management area. Maybe even an abandoned railroad. There's a wealth of pleasant short walks near by. Just stir your bones a bit and look for them.

What do you take with you? A friend. A kid or three. A dog. Somebody to share with. An old pair of pants and an old shirt, a pair of sneakers, a sweater tied around your middle and a roll of hard candies in your pocket. It's not a very inter-esting list.

And so you did it, and it was pleasant, even fun, in a low-keyed way. Try it again next week. If you come back then wishing you could have stayed longer, and thinking about what was over the next little rise, it's about time you went down to see the people who were helpful to you over the telephone. Leave your check-book and your credit cards at home, and outfit your wallet with an eighteen dollar bill. Tell the folks there what you've been doing, thank them for their assistance on the phone, and ask them to show you a few daybags in the $12.50 price range. They may be out of bags of that sort. A good shop will tell you when they're out, and more than likely will advise you about what you need. They may even call their competition across town to see if they have something in stock to save you the hassle.

1

The daybag is the simplest form of pack. At this price, it won't have bells and whistles on it. It won't even have padded shoulder straps, but don't worry about that. You won't be carrying more than seven pounds, anyway.

Even at this price level, you'll find a surprisingly wide array of designs to choose from. A common type is a squatty little bag that looks like a pumpkin with a purse on top. This design offers the most room for the money, but this may be a mixed blessing if you overstuff it. The one pictured is an excellent example of the type, the Sierra Designs Simplex. Packs in this price range are almost inevitably made of a sturdy nylon duck that weighs about eight ounces per yard. The fabric is coated on one side with a urethane elastomer to seal it against water. For the record, you can't waterproof nylon with a surfactant like Scotchguard. It must be coated. To simplify your life, we'll call this fabric *pack fabric* or *pack cloth* throughout the book. The commonest pack cloth used in the industry is called Parapac. If you see that name, you'll know what it is.

SIERRA DESIGNS SIMPLEX

Let's look more closely at our little nylon pumpkin. It's an open sack that closes with a drawstring and cord lock. The purse on the top is its hat, as it were. The simplest daybag would be protected against rain and dust by a simple nylon flap. This little zippered pocket is most handy for items such as maps, a compass, insect repellent, sun glasses, and film.

While this type of bag is pretty standard, it still pays to check out its construction. Is the cover, be it purse or flap, really well sewn into the pack, or does it look like it'll pull off if you look at it cross-eyed? Are the shoulder straps sewn on top and bottom well? Is the arrangement for holding the flap down fastened securely? And finally, does the pack seem comfortable? All the technical details and fine sewing in the world won't do you a bit of good if the pack binds under your arms, bites your shoulders, or hangs wrong. It fits? Even with a few pounds of trail guides stuffed inside it? Great. But before you decide on that design, take a look at a few other types as well:

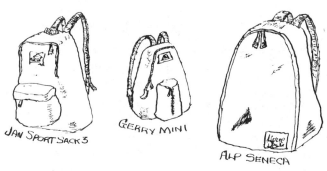

JAN SPORT SACKS

GERRY MINI

ALP SENECA

There's a certain similarity among all these bags, but there are meaningful differences. The Alp, with its suitcase zipper, is the easiest to get into, but the design depends entirely on the zipper for the integrity of the front panel. This shouldn't be a major worry, though. Contemporary zippers are tough, reliable items. The Jan Sport design offers the convenience of a zippered front pocket, but access to the major part of your storage area is through a relatively small opening. You'll have to empty the pack to get at what's on the bottom — and what you want always seems to be on the bottom. The Gerry Mini is an example of the teardrop design commonly seen in more expensive daybags. This design permits a little freer movement in the shoulders at the expense of pack access.

I have my own preference in daybag style. I carry a teardrop bag that's divided into an upper and a lower compartment. It has padded shoulder straps, a waistband to keep the pack close to my body, a heavy leather bottom to resist abrasion, a 10-ounce Cordura nylon body, and a tab and strap for securing an ice axe. It's meant for hard travelin'. You don't need it, and I really don't most of the time. Besides, it costs twice what the less complex ones do.

MY BAG, IF YOU'RE CURIOUS.

What I use shouldn't be your concern, though. There are maybe thirty well-made useful daybags on the market in this $12.50 price range. They'll all look more or less like one of the bags illustrated above, and any one of them will do the job. Pick what looks good to you, what feels good on you, and what you think is most useful.

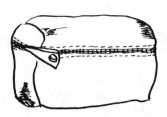 AN EXPOSED
ZIPPER MAY
LEAK IN A
HARD RAIN.

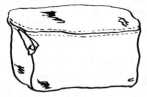 A COVERED
ZIPPER GIVES
BETTER RAIN
PROTECTION.

 THIS STITCH
PATTERN HOLDS
WELL ON
NYLON STRAPS.

 THIS DOESN'T
HOLD UP WELL.

 DOUBLE D-RINGS
WILL SLIP IN USE
AS SHOULDER
STRAP ADJUSTERS.

 TABLER BUCKLES
DON'T SLIP, AND
ADJUST QUICKLY.

You've blown about thirteen bucks after taxes. The next thing you want is a cheap vinyl poncho that will keep you dry in a rain for about two dollars. That's cheap protection. They tear easily, but you're not waddling around brushbound — you're on open trails, so rest easy. Your last purchase is a one pint plastic water bottle. My favorite kind is a ribbed one from Austria, with a red stopper and a green cap. It's about a buck. How about that? You will have enough left from the eighteen dollar bill to buy a six-pack of Ballantine ale on the way home! That's good money management.

Now you're pretty well set for long walks in easy terrain. You have something that holds water and a daybag to put it in. Your sweater can come off your waist and go into the daybag, too, and your roll of hard candy can be beefed up a bit with some cheddar cheese, a torpedo roll, and some pepperoni. Off you go!

After a few more trips, you'll spot some deficiencies in this outfit. The first one will be footgear. Those old sneakers were fine for the traces through the reforestation area, and good on the abandoned railroad bed, but that trail up to the fire tower you walked yesterday was pretty rocky in spots, and steep, too. A little better traction would have helped; so would a little more beef in the sole of the shoe. Your feet weren't exactly sore, but you knew they were there, hanging from your ankles during the last half mile. Yep, you could use some boots.

The mountain was just fine, though. That close to home, too. Who'd believe it. And that pond off to the north, glistening in the slantwise sunlight like a tiny diamond set in a cluster of emeralds. The young woman who helped you select your daybag mentioned that pond when she told you about the trail to the fire tower. She said there was a trail into it that followed a stream most of the way. It's about a seventeen mile round trip. Could you do it in a day? No, you realize you're not in that kind of shape yet, but it'd be kind of nice to stay overnight in there. She mentioned some fairly good trout fishing, besides. Hmmm. . . .

When you start musing that way, you're a backpacker. You may not know it right now, but you are. It's going to use up a lot of your time, a fair chunk of your money, and many, many calories. This book can't do a thing about the calories. It can help you spend your trail time more pleasantly, and it can help you select the gear you need to see that pond, and the next pond, and the pond out beyond the horizon that you just know is there.

There's a lot of technical chatter in the pages that follow. It's there to help you make decisions when you're faced with a lot of alternatives. It may be more than you need, but I ran a wilderness outfitting shop for six years, and I always believed that if I gave a customer the whole story, he could make up his own mind without pressure.

I'm an upstate New Yorker. I've done some hiking in the West, and I've served my apprenticeship in the Whites and the Greens, but the Adirondacks are home to me. They're typical of the climate we Easterners face in the mountains from Maine to Georgia in spring, summer and fall. Chillier than most, but typical. This book is about Eastern hiking, and gear for Eastern hiking. It's maybe less of a weight watcher's book than those written by Westerners. We don't have high elevations, long approach marches and permanent snowfields to worry about. No way. We have roots, rocks, cripplebush, puckerbrush, rain, snow, the greasiest mud in Christendom, and an occasional day of splendor that I wouldn't trade for the whole damn Sierra from Banner Peak to Williamson Basin.

We're not going to touch winter hiking here, except for those occasional snow showers in August. Winter is a world of its own and a volume all by itself. It's crisp, abstract, silent and dangerous. We're talking summer, with a few random scoots back into spring and ahead into autumn. That pond's still there; you haven't seen it yet, have you? It's getting late in the year. If you're going to get those new boots broken in before the snow flies, we'd better go get 'em now. Let's move out!

2. THE SOLE OF IT

> *"A hiking boot's nothing but a sneaker with chutzpah."*
> —Mike Chessler

All backpacking begins and ends with the feet. This should be as obvious as pouring sand in a rathole, but it evidently isn't. I see them every weekend, staggering into an Adirondack leanto, with three hundred dollars worth of gear on their backs and an old pair of street shoes on their feet, or limp, rumpsprung "huntin' boots". And, my God, are they hurting! You never hear complaints about aching backs, but cries "Oh, my feet are killing me!" waver through the North Country valleys like the wails of ghostly mountain lions.

Use your head, and protect your feet. I'd advise you to begin your major equipment purchase with a well-fitted, well-made pair of boots. March on down to your friendly local outfitter, tell him you want a boot suitable for general backpacking in the Northeast, and put yourself in his hands. Trust him — but not completely. Go armed with a little knowledge of how boots are built, and why they're built that way.

Let's begin with the human foot. I'm not a podiatrist, and chances are that you aren't either, so I'm not going to get unduly technical. But if a boot is to fit you properly, you should be aware of certain anatomical landmarks. The first ones are the 1st and 5th metatarsal heads, the areas just behind the great toe and the little toe, at the points where they bend. This is the widest part of the foot. Next is the longitudinal arch, which begins just ahead of the weight-bearing surface of the heel and extends forward to a line across the metatarsal heads.

Next are the two bones of the ankle, and last (and not least, since it's the commonest point of irritation), the heel. You should also bear in mind that there are four distinct "arches" that must be fitted. There is an arch across the instep, and one across the metatarsals. The longitudinal arch follows the inside (great toe side) of the foot, and there is a smaller outer arch that must also be accommodated. To account for all these variances, bootmakers form the uppers of boots over a foot form called a "last". Last measurements are derived from statistical surveys of the critical dimensions of human feet.

In America, the largest statistical sample for men is, of course, the records of the U.S. Army. There are notable distinctions in lasts. The European foot is generally "square" — i.e. wider in the heel in relationship to the ball than is the American foot, and shorter in the toe than the American foot. Accordingly, if you have a typical American foot (wide at the ball, narrow at the heel, and long-toed) a French, German or Italian last (and *these* are different, too!) will generally be loose in the heel, will crowd the small toe considerably, and will be too long in the arch.

7

Most European makers who export build on American lasts — Fabiano and Lowa being the most widely distributed in the Northeast — and America's makers who have some boots built in Europe also build American lasts. There are differences, too, in American lasts. The Fabiano, for example, is narrower in the heel than the Lowa by a fair amount. An "American" last may be a misnomer, in that each boot-maker modifies his lasts to accommodate what he sees as the American hiker's foot. After many years of outfitting, I've found that the easiest boots to fit successfully have been Fabiano, Vasque and Lowa, in that order.

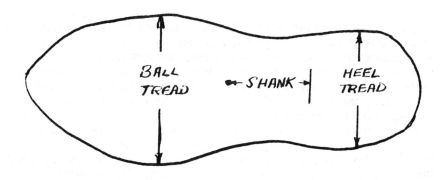

This information should be greeted by you with an only fairly interested nod. I don't know what your foot looks like. Statistically, one of these three boots will most likely do the job, but you may have a very French foot, and a Galibier may be ideal for you. I greatly admire Galibier's bootmaking, especially the superb Super Guide (Super RD), but my feet would curdle if I wore a pair for over a half-mile. At any rate, try on various boots — most outfitters carry more than one line — and buy the one that's most comfortable. Don't be hornswoggled by an "expert" friend who says that "so-and-so's boots are terrible." They may be, FOR HIM. But they may be ideal for you. Let your feet and your outfitter's knowledge of how a given model of boot will fit after a little use, be the determining factor.

What should your feet look for? "Comfort" is a difficult word to define, especially because a good, sturdy boot is not limp. It will feel strange to you, and if it feels strange, it will not be comfortable as an old pair of slippers might be called comfortable. The boot should fit snugly above the ankle, but it should not cut into the flesh. A heavy boot usually has a padded collar or scree cuff to alleviate this problem. Lighter-weight boots may or may not have scree cuffs, and those without may "bite" you for a few minutes. Generally, the leather is sufficiently pliable in the lightweight boot so as to break in readily and conform to your ankle. It is imperative that the boot's arch-length be accurate. The ball of the foot should rest in the ball of the boot, and the boot should be snugly set against the inside longitudinal arch. There must be space in front of the toes, and a common method of fitting seems to work here. With the boot unlaced, and your toes touching the end of the toe box, there should be a half inch — a finger's thickness is a good approximation — between your heel and the heel cup of the boot.

Proper width is a bit subtler to analyze. Again, a sturdy hiking boot is relatively firm when it's new, and it resists being moved around by your foot. Accordingly, it's far too easy to buy a boot that's too wide, because your feet are aware of the heavy, relatively unyielding uppers. In general, there should be sufficient width for each toe to lie normally on the innersole of the boot without crowding, crossing, or compressing. Except in a heavy mountaineering boot, if you push your thumbs together on the top of the boot at the metatarsal head, you should be able to produce a tiny "ripple" of leather. Too much ripple and the boot is too loose. Your feet will slide around as you walk, and you'll blister. No ripple, and the boot will constrict circulation as your feet spread when you're walking. The counter pocket must hold your heel firmly in place as well. This, again, is not easy to assess. The midsole structure of a heavy boot resists bending, and the resultant force tends to make the boot slip on the heel. If there's less than a quarter inch of heel lift, chances are that the heel will stay firmly in place as the sole structure loosens up a bit. Don't be afraid to take a lot of time to select a boot — and much of that time should be spent walking around the store, because this is one purchase where your intellect should permit itself to be overruled by feedback from your feet.

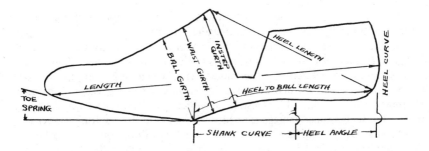

A TYPICAL ROCKER LAST FOR A HIKING BOOT

So much for fitting. Except to mention that boots should be fitted over the socks you'll be wearing with them later. My own preference is for a very thin wool-liner sock (the Wigwam Mojave or the North Cape, specifically) and a North Cape stretch raggwool sock over that. If you dislike wool next to your hide, use an olefin sock or a *thin* cotton sock. But more on this later. Let's first get the boots.

Finding a boot that fits is one problem. Finding one that fits and that doesn't fall apart after three days is another problem. Let's look at what a boot is made of, how it's put together, and develop a set of criteria for evaluating any boot you may be tempted to buy. To begin with, boots are made of leather, usually cattle hide. A "hide", by the way, refers to mature animals, whereas "skin" refers to immature animals or small animals. Thus, horsehide and cowhide, as opposed to goatskin and calfskin. Conversion of Old Bessie's hide into leather fit for a mountain boot is an involved, time-consuming series of processes to remove excess fats, flesh and hair, and convert the hide chemically into a stable substance that will not rot readily.

Tanning is only one of the steps in the process, but is one of the key processes in that the tanning method determines, to a great extent, the "feel" of the leather. Tanning may be done in two steps. It is common to tan a hide, and after wringing, split the hide and retan it, usually in a tanning bath that imparts different properties. The hide (more properly called leather at that point) is dyed and fatliquored (moisturized and lubricated) at the same time as it is retanned. There are three commonly used tanning methods. The commonest is chrome tanning, with soluble chromium salts. The result is a very pliable leather that dries soft when wet, but does not hold shape outstandingly well.

For 5,000 years the only process used for tanning was called "bark tannins". This is actually vegetable tanning, using vegatable materials from plants and trees. Hemlock bark was the commonest bark tannin in use in America, and the stripping of hemlock bark was a staple source of income in pioneer times. Vegetable tanned leather is typically firmer than chrome-tanned leather, and dries stiff as — well, stiff as a dried boot. As neither process is exactly perfect for a sturdy mountain boot, most leather is combination-tanned, using chromium salts and bark tannin. Certain other ingredients are typically used, either here or during retanning. Among these are silicones or wax for water repellency, or non-hydroscopic oils to add flexibility and to close the pores against water.

A full hide is thick, far too thick for most boot applications, so it must be split before use, typically between the tanning and retanning operations. At this point, we can consider three basic types of boot leather — full grain, roughout, and split. Full grain (sometimes called "shell grain") leather is leather with the hair removed, but the natural surface remaining, complete with healed range scars and fly bites. The natural surface is the densest part of the leather, the toughest, and the most inherently water-repellent. It is also most subject to abrasion damage. One way to protect the shell against damage is to turn it inside out; the resulting leather is called roughout. It may have a sueded (brushed nap) finish, but it is most emphatically NOT suede, which is a thin, brushed-nap leather made of a split — the inside of a hide.

A third type of leather is called "split leather." It is almost always sueded, and is what's left over after the top grain has been skived away. With a looser fiber than the top grain, it will stretch more. Lightweight boots use this leather, and those bootmaker's aberrations called "ladies' trail shoes." The quality of a split may range from very good for its purpose to absolute junk. There are ways to work with splits, however, that make them very acceptable. The best is to "stuff" the leather during the fatliquoring part of processing, and then back the split with a reinforcing doubler. This is a costly process, and to my knowledge the Fabiano lightweight is the only boot built in its class that uses this type of split-leather. How can you tell a lightweight roughout from a split? Not easily, unless you know the bootmaker, or your outfitter does. Since the hiking shoe has become a minor fashion item, there are chamber pots full of ersatz boots made of cheap split leather on the market. None of them are worth the powder to blow them up — and it wouldn't take much. The most popular, the Dunham Wafflestomper, is known in the outfitting trade as "Dunham's Disposable." 'Nuff said. All bootmakers, by the way, use splits for vamp linings, scree cuffs, and sock liners.

Now that we have some leather, let's build a boot to see how it's put together.

The sole goes on last, but most neophyte backpackers come stomping in all charged up about Vibram soles. If it's got Vibram soles, it must be the real article. This is nonsense. The Vibram sole, designed by mountaineer Vitale Bramanti, is a composition sole whose pattern is a molded copy of traditional Tricouni hobnails. It's a good bootsole. So is the St. Moritz, which I have on my boots. At any rate, all of the composition soles come in several hardness grades. You want the black, which is the hardest. It also leaves carbon marks on floors, but that's a small price to pay for the right gear. In general, the middleweight and heavyweight (mountaineering) boots use the so-called Montagna sole (deep cleats and a thick substrate), and the lightweights use the Roccia sole (shallow cleats, thin substrate). The St. Moritz is equivalent to the Montagna Vibram, except that it has a half-clinker pattern under the instep, which I like on wet Northeastern roots. Some people don't. While the sole is important, the point to remember is that it doesn't have to say Vibram to be good, despite what you may hear.

The sole is not attached directly to the upper on any boot worth considering. The sole is glued on, or glued and screwed on, after the basic boot is completed — i.e., the upper fastened to the midsole structure, or the midsole and insole, if it's a Goodyear or a Norwegian welt.

Let's look at boot cutaways for a second. The first pattern you see is the Goodyear (or perfect) welt, probably the optimum welt for heavy boots.

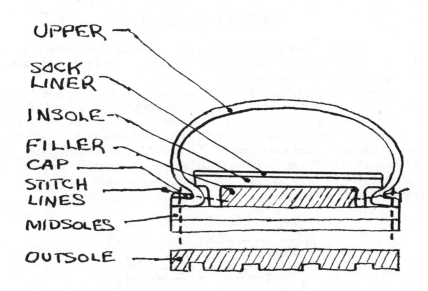

UPPER

SOCK LINER

INSOLE

FILLER

CAP

STITCH LINES

MIDSOLES

OUTSOLE

GOODYEAR WELT

Initially, the upper is side-stitched to the insole, which is filled with either a rubber form or a cork-and-cement mixture. The midsoles are glued to each other and to the insole-filler, the welt glued to the midsole, and the welt and midsoles stitched together. The outsole, or the sole as most people know it, is then attached to the boot.

A variation of this welt is called the Norwegian (or reverse) welt, which looks like this:

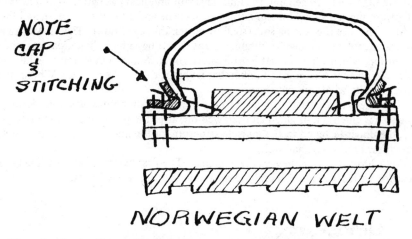

NOTE
CAP
$\frac{1}{3}$
STITCHING

NORWEGIAN WELT

Note that in the Norwegian welt, the upper is slant-stitched to the insole and then rolled out, to be double stitched to the midsoles. There may or may not be a cap, although one is shown in the illustration.

Another common construction method, and very commonly seen on the better lightweight boots, is the Littleway, which permits a very closely-trimmed sole with little or no overhang. It's seldom used on medium or heavy boots except for a few models of Pivettas and Vasques, and there are those who question its durability for heavy boots. It *looks* dubious to me, but Pivetta and Vasque boots hold together, so I guess it works. It does result in a stitch line around the outside of the foot that's often ill-covered by the sock liner, however, and can cause some tender-skinned souls some discomfort.

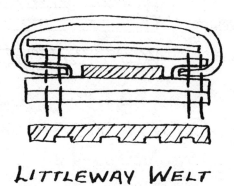

LITTLEWAY WELT

As to a choice of these construction methods, there really isn't one. Most hiking boots and mountaineering boots are made with a Goodyear or a Norwegian welt; most lightweight boots use Littleway construction. If you want something beside a lightweight, it will almost certainly be welted.

Various good people who spend their lives hiking in the dry Sierras, and who write books on backpacking that are swallowed whole by us damnfool Easterners, warn of the dangers of water pouring into a welted boot through the thread holes, and, so help me, they believe it. Well, it just ain't so, no matter what you've read. One, the leather will swell a bit around the threads. Two, most welts either have a thread cap or are sealed with a resin compound. Three, if the two above were not true, a coat of a wax-based waterproofer like SNO-SEAL would keep things dry. So much for experts.

Now let's look at what goes into these little diagrams. The sole (outsole) we've already talked about. The midsole (or midsoles as the case may be) is typically of leather, and will range from 5-iron thickness (an iron is 1/48 of an inch, a charmingly archaic unit of measure perpetuated by the leather goods trade) on a lightweight to as heavy as 12-iron on a mountaineering boot. There may be several midsoles, all of leather, or one may be of composition rubber, usually about 6-iron thickness. The insole also varies in thickness from 4-iron to as much as 8, and is manufactured in two ways. The most common by far is the normal sheet of leather with the stitching rib glued to it.

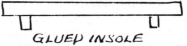

GLUED INSOLE

Less common, and more desirable if it's not shaved too thin, is a one-piece insole with the stitching rib skived out. Obviously, there's no glue line to fail. Obviously, also, is the hazard that some overworked operator skived the rib too thinly.

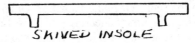

SKIVED INSOLE

The area under the insole is either filled with a ground cork and glue mastic, or rubber, or in the case of some super-sturdy mountaineering boots, a fiberglass filler-cum-midsole. The shank, of course, also fits in this area. Shanks are typically of spring steel. They function as a "backbone" for the boot, and aid in providing a pivot for the hinging-type flex of a bootsole. The latter is not terribly significant with a medium to heavy boot, as the sole flexes little anyway, and the sole is rockered (just like the rocker on a rocking chair) to aid in walking without fully flexing the sole. Some boots utilize a laminated wooden shank, notably Raichle and Dolomite, with the idea that there is less heat loss and a smoother flex pattern to the shank. Lowa uses an almost full-length molded nylon shank, carefully "tuned" to boot size and boot style. Again, they claim better flex control and less heat loss. Most manufacturers use a steel shank. It would seem that shank material, like filler material, is less a determiner of the boot's performance than the general integrity of the manufacturer and the quality of the materials used throughout the boot. Raichle and Dolomite make good boots. So does Lowa. So do Fabiano and Vasque, and they use steel shanks.

We live with different design concepts in all backpacking gear, and there will always be heated debates about design concepts and materials. The fact still remains — well made, carefully made, pridefully made gear usually means well-functioning gear. It's that simple. Suffice it to say that I've owned well-designed boots that fell apart in no time, and I've owned a pair of Lowa Alpspitz for five years and they're still healthy. I also wear the Fabiano Cragman mountaineering boot, rather radically different from the Lowas in design and construction, that have seen hard use for two years and are in immaculate condition. If I had let myself get "locked in" to buying a design concept or a sole pattern (the Lowas have Vibram Montagna soles, the big Fabianos have St. Moritz's) or a particular type of leather (the Lowa is a roughout, the Fabiano a Scotch Grain smoothout, called *"stompato"* by the Italian bootmakers) or a particular shank (the Lowa is nylon, the Fabiano steel) or a particular welt (the Lowa is Norwegian, the Fabiano is Goodyear) or soles fastened with screws all over (the Lowa is stapled, the Fabiano has screws in the heel only) or a particular lacing system (the Lowa is speedlaced for a bit, then uses hooks, and the Fabiano is all hooks), I might not have bought either boot. As it was, I simply bought a heavy, well-made boot that fitted both my purposes and my feet, and I turned up with two pairs of winners, both very different.

It's obvious that the stitching in all parts of a boot is critical, but it is nowhere more critical than in the fastening of the upper to the insole and midsole. A seam that pops a stitch on the upper is a nuisance only — a failed welt stitch can cause the boot to self-destruct. Needless to say, this stitching, as all stitching on a boot, should be done with synthetic thread. Cotton rots in time. Dacron and nylon don't rot. Your better boots (and some miserable ones) are generally sewn with synthetic thread. It's more expensive, and it's certainly more difficult to sew with (maintaining proper tension with synthetic thread is a horror), but the better makers live with the hassle. You think for a minute that Willy Sacre at Vasque wants his boots falling apart on the trail? Or Eddie Fabiano? Or any other builder seriously committed to the hiking and mountaineering trade? Not on your tintype, Lucinda! Word travels like crownfire through the leantos and into the backpacking shops, and the next thing the manufacturer knows, he's reduced to selling his boots at glorified patio shops and a few chain drugstores in resort areas. Boots are sewn with synthetic thread. Period. If they're not, walk away. Fast!

Now let's look at the upper of a boot. While the sole structure keeps the boot together, and provides the firm platform for walking, the upper is where your feet live. Right off the bat, it's evident that a multiplicity of seams in an upper will cause a boot to flex in strange and wondrous ways that bear only a dim resemblance to what your foot wants to do. Therefore, the fewer seams the better. The fewer pieces actually encasing the foot the better. I can think of no first-rate boot in any price or weight range that is now sewn with a one-piece upper. Generally, the upper is joined at the heel, and the seam is covered with a cap, called a back stay. In some designs, the upper is joined at the inside of the foot, at about the arch. This obviates the necessity for the heel seam, and, in theory, eliminates any possible chafing of the heel or the Achilles tendon from a seam. In practice, the seam is rolled, capped, and padded inside, and a heel counter adds additional protection; so the problem is largely theoretical.

As I've said, each bootmaker has his own way of working. All the good ones have definite similarities, as well as their own idiosyncrasies. Let's examine cutaway drawings of three specimen boots — a lightweight boot of Littleway construction, a middleweight with a Goodyear welt, and a very heavy-duty mountaineering boot, also with a Goodyear welt.

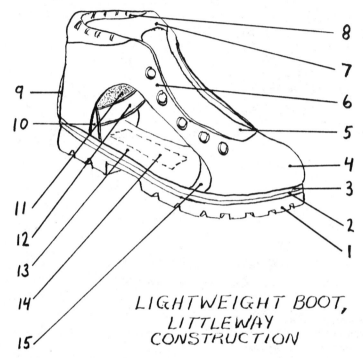

LIGHTWEIGHT BOOT,
LITTLEWAY
CONSTRUCTION

1. Vibram sole and heel, black Rocciabloc
2. 5-iron leather midsole)
3. 5-iron rubber midsole) may be a simple 8-iron rubber midsole
4. Fibre box toe for protection
5. Padded tongue, bellows-sewn for water protection
6. One-piece upper, 5-ounce full-grain roughout, combination tanned with silicones
7. Foam-padded screecuff covered with goatskin. Not common lightweights, and not necessary. But nice.
8. Full split leather lining
9. Back stay
10. Molded counter of leather fibre and neoprene
11. Ankle pad — 1/4 to 1/2 inch of foam rubber covering ankles on both sides.
12. Lining
13. Insole with sock liner. Should be of leather; may be of cellulose. If it's cellulose, it must be so stated, by law. Sock liner usually of split leather or goatskin.
14. Spring steel shank
15. Vamp liner of split leather. Not always present, but useful in that it helps the boot retain its shape better. It may or may not be more comfortable.

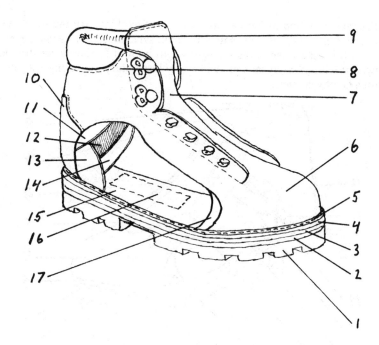

MIDDLEWEIGHT BOOT,
GOODYEAR WELT

Key, middleweight boots
1. Vibram Montagnabloc sole and heel. Screwed in place in the heel as well as bonded.
2. 6-iron rubber midsole doubler
3. 8-iron leather midsole
4. Rubber filler between insole and midsole
5. Goodyear welt. You'd see another row of stitching slanting inward if it was a Norwegian welt. In some boots, the welt stitching is capped with either a plastic compound or a thin full-grain cap cemented in place.
6. Heavy-duty toe cap of leather fiber and neoprene
7. Padded, preformed tongue, bellows-sewn.
8. One-piece upper, 7 oz. full grain roughout, combination tanned with silicones
9. Scree cuff, goatskin-covered foam rubber
10. Reinforced backstay and counter pocket
11. Doubler of split leather. Provides extra ankle support, helps boot maintain shape. A doubler, which may appear anywhere, is, as the name implies, a second piece of leather (or rubber, in a midsole) cut to the same pattern and fitted inside of (or beneath) the primary piece as reinforcement.
12. Foam rubber ankle pad, 1/2 inch thick
13. Impregnated leather counter, pre-molded
14. Split leather lining
15. 8-iron leather insole, glued rib
16. Spring steel shank, longer and stiffer than in lightweight boot
17. Leather-lined vamp

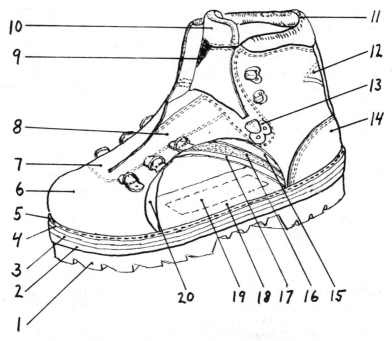

HEAVYWEIGHT MOUNTAIN BOOT

GOODYEAR OR NORWEGIAN WELT

Key for heavyweight boot
1. St. Moritz lug sole, extra screw fasteners at heel, toe and shank
2. 8-iron leather midsole
3. 8-iron leather midsole doubler
4. 10-iron filler
5. Goodyear welt
6. Heavy-duty fibre boxtoe
7. One piece upper, 12 oz. full grain roughout, combination tanned, wax finished
8. Ski flap closure and bellows gusset for additional weather protection.
9. Velcro tab to align tongue; matching tab on inside quarter
10. Preformed, padded, hinged tongue
11. Scree cuff, foam rubber covered with goatskin
12. Hinge to permit fore and aft flexing of boot. Some like it; some don't. I do.
13. Heavy duty, double rived hooks – this one is a locking hook to permit variable lacing of the boot for climbing or for the approach march.
14. Double reinforced counter pocket
15. 6-iron leather board doubler surrounding ankle
16. Foam padding, 1/2-inch thick, for ankle protection
17. Split leather quarter lining
18. Insole of 10-iron leather, skived rib
19. Molded nylon shank
20. Split leather vamp liner

Bear in mind that no one boot is likely to have each and every feature of the illustration. Some weights of leather may vary, some midsole constructions will vary, welts will vary, and on the big mountaineering boots you may find all sorts of devices for hinging, closing, and double-closing the great, heavy brutes. But, while any one good boot may not look like these, there should be enough points of similarity, or good reasons given for the dissimilarity by the outfitter, to enable you to evaluate the construction of any boot you're interested in.

If you're an average hiker, you'll snub the mountaineering boot like the plague. These big dudes are real high points of the bootmaker's art, but you don't need them. Unless you have a big sackful of loose bread to throw away for a Vasque Glacier, Fabiano Cragman, Lowa Civetta, Galibier Super Guide or Karl Molitor Eisboot (which may, along with the LaRoux Harlin model, be the crème de la crème), forget it, man. Stash those dollars and spend them slowly on some little luxury like an occasional bottle of Ballantine India Pale Ale.

If day tripping and occasional backpacking is what you're into, or think you'll be into, consider the lightweight. If you're trucking around in the Whites or the Adirondacks, consider the mediumweight. I'm skinny,with bony feet and walk fast (gracelessly) and pack heavy. I'm well past 35, hustling toward Nirvana, and I like my little luxuries. My Mountain Red comes in a poly bottle rather than in the original glass bottle, to be sure, but I still opt to carry it. Add a few more goodies and a fairly heavy, BIG two-man mountaineering tent (an old Alp T-400, now called the Snowline – a great tent but surely no 4 1/2 pound wonder) and my bony feet need the protection of a heavy boot. For my needs, with my own set of problems, a boot like the Lowa Alpspitz, Fabiano 772 Mountain Master, or the Vasque Whitney is satisfactory, and these are in the light-heavyweight class. At the other extreme, my wife would cheerfully backpack in tennis sneakers, although she broke down and bought a pair of Fabiano 365's, a Littleway-built roughout lightweight, and a fine value even in the opinion of other boot makers.

At any rate, try on the lightweights and the middleweights, and shuffle around in each, preferably with a pack on your back to splay out your feet a bit. If you can live with the lightweight, do it. It's less money, lighter, and easier to break in. On the other hand, because the leather is thinner and less dense, it will not stay dry as well as a mediumweight of good quality. Don't let this deter you. Chances of keeping your feet dry in the Northeast are pretty minimal unless you're wearing a brute boot or waders. And a fresh, dry change of socks will dry out the lightweight pretty well.

So-o-o-o, let's recap boot construction techniques. If you want a lightweight boot, look for the following:

1. Littleway construction. Welted is okay, of course, but there are no welted lightweights to my knowledge. Injection molded construction? NO!
2. Black Vibran Roccia sole or equivalent (color is an index of hardness – carbon black makes the soles harder).
3. Full grain uppers, or a heavy split leather
4. Roughout construction
5. One-piece uppers with backstay
6. Synthetic thread throughout
7. Lines quarter and vamp

8. Fibre toe box
9. Premolded counter
10. Steel shank or equivalent
11. Padding for the ankles
12. Bellows tongue or ski flaps
13. Minimum 5-iron midsole — may be rubber or leather
14. Leather insole

I like hooks. Some like eyelets. Others like speedlaces. I also like scree cuffs, but I don't think they're necessary on a lightweight. You may want them, but in six years as an outfitter, I have had only one complaint about a chafed tendon from a lightweight without a scree cuff, and that came from a person who was so badly deconditioned that her ankles swelled badly when she walked any distance. She was persistent, though, and hung on until she got the machine back together. The trouble with the boots vanished like the mists of a summer morn.

For my money, the only lightweights that I'd consider are the little Fabiano or Vasque's Edelweiss. My chief gripe against the Edelweiss is a cellulose insole and an unreinforced split leather in the quarter, although I like the midsole construction, the scree cuff, and the fit and "feel" of the boot. The Fabianos use a leather insole, and the split upper is reinforced. The Vasque comes in men's and ladies' models, three widths of each, while the Fabiano comes in three widths only, but built on an excellently conceived combination last that seems, from my experience, to fit beautifully for all but super-square feet. The Fabiano is confusing. The boot comes in five colors. The 365 is gray. In the past it had a heavier shank and a thicker midsole than its flashier pals, but now they're made all the same.

If you're looking at mediumweight boots, there are certain material and construction criteria you should look for.

1. In a mediumweight boot I'd be inclined toward welted construction, but there are a few Littleway-built mediumweights on the market with good reputation. Don't pass them over without a thought.
2. Black Vibram Montagna sole or St. Moritz sole. Glued soles without screws are perfectly acceptable.
3. Full grain leather uppers, of 8 ounce leather.
4. Roughout construction preferred. This isn't mandatory, but it does protect the grain against the rough Northeast terrain.
5. One-piece uppers with backstay and counter reinforcement
6. Synthetic threat throughout
7. Lined quarter and vamp
8. Fibre toe box
9. Premolded counter
10. Steel shank or equivalent
11. Ankle padding
12. Bellows tongue or ski flaps
13. Doubler in quarter, to protect ankles and to retain shape of boot.
14. Leather insole, 8 or 10 iron
15. Midsole and doubler, combined thickness of 12 iron. May be two 6-iron leathers, two 6-iron rubbers or (usually) one of each.
16. Padded scree cuff

There are many, many middleweight boots on the market. Selection of one can be confusing, and when you're asked to shell out fifty dollars or more for one, the decision becomes a bit more critical. Probably the two commonest boots in this class in the Northeast are the Vasque Hiker II and the Fabiano 791. They are rather different boots in concept, appearance, and feel. The Hiker II looks like what you'd think a mountaineering boot should look like, while the 791 looks like an overgrown lightweight. In this case, looks are monumentally deceiving. The Brown Fuzzy, as it came to be called in our shop, is one rugged boot, despite its tender appearance, and I will unhesitatingly recommend it for the Northeast hiker. This is not based on experience with one or two boots, either. This is based on having sent maybe *2000* of them into the field when I was an outfitter. There were a few bad ones — three, maybe — but I have a lot of respect for this shoe. My customers used them for everything from trekking in Nepal to first ascents in the Wind Rivers to after-ski boots at Mad River Glen. I can't see you going wrong with either boot. The Lowa Scout is well regarded in the category as well, and Raichle seems to have made a great effort to get their boots out into the market place of late. In the past, they were hard to find. Their reputation is certainly good, and the boots I've seen from them look to be well made, but I haven't torn one apart, so I don't know. Trak has also entered the market with a solid-looking boot line.

I'm not going to get further into the superboot category. While I may wear them for heavy packing, I have my own set of needs, and they're probably not yours. If you feel that you need a superboot, I'd certainly suggest that you look at the Fabiano Leader, the Lowa Civetta and the Vasque Glacier. There are others, to be sure, and I suspect that at this level, all boots are good. But I know these three well, and I know that they work.

Now that you've gotten your boots, you'd best set out to make friends with them. Please do not hop into your new boots and walk twenty miles in them the first day. They will resent it and will turn your feet to jelly to show their resentment. Wear them around the house for a few days first, to let the soles break in a bit, and to permit the uppers to conform to your foot. Be watchful of the laces at this point. Keep the boots laced firmly. The laces will slip as the leather stretches (or resists stretching), and a new boot that's loose, especially a heavier one, can generate enough heat to produce a blister in a surprisingly short time. I won't say that blisters are inevitable. They rarely bother me, but then I walk a lot and wear boots a lot. No, I didn't get married in mountain boots. I changed out of them into dress shoes shortly before, and was delighted to change back again.

As sure as God made hot summers in Kansas, some damn fool is going to tell you that standing in a creek with new boots and wearing them dry is the only to break in boots. It's an old Army trick, and it worked with the Army shoes of WWI vintage. It was an invention born of necessity. The Army shoe, while well-lasted (the Munson combination last is a lovely one for the narrow-heeled Americano), was often pinched in the throat and drawn too tightly in the spade, because the contractors could knock down a little material that way. Leather stretches when wet, so the doughboy soaked his boots, pulled on extra socks, and wore the boots until dry to stretch the throat and spade of the boot so it wouldn't cut his toes off with each step. This is not only unnecessary today but it can also be detrimental to the health of the boot, to say nothing of your feet.

Dry socks are the answer to healthy feet on the trail. As I've said, I prefer the combination of a *light* wool Wigwam Mojave or North Cape liner sock (get them a bit large — they run a bit skimpy in cut) and a North Cape stretch ragg oversock. Wool is what you need for cushioning, for breatheability, and for perspiration absorption. If you're allergic to wool, wear a cotton or a synthetic liner sock. Some people swear by silk liners. They're expensive, fragile, and in my observation, tend to encourage blisters — possibly because most people wear them until they're soaking wet. "Dry" is the word. When your innersock gets wet from sweat, change socks and rinse out the used pair if you're going to reuse them on a long trip. This isn't a cleanliness kick, it's just good sense. Salt, in heavy concentrations, is an irritant. Rinsing the socks gets rid of the accumulated salt.

Except for the brute boots, it's difficult to keep any boot perfectly dry. A rubber boot will stay dry, but you'll be walking in a small, smelly puddle of sweat inside. A well made leather boot can be kept surprisingly dry by the application of a good waterproofing treatment. Sno-Seal, a wax-based dressing developed for ski boots years ago, does a good job if you follow instructions, and a better job if you don't. I'm leery of heat around boots, so I just smear the stuff on, rub it in well, and forget it. There are several brush-on silicones that work well, particularly on the brushed finish roughouts. Sno-Seal will mat down a brushed finish, and the silicones won't. Neither will soften a boot, which is generally desirable. I've found that mink oil works well on lighter leathers, but the big boots respond best to Sno-Seal or to Tierowa, an old-time German dressing that's essentially tallow with silicone. It's excellent stuff, but hard to find. Peter Limmer, the East's renowned custom bootmaking firm in Intervale, New Hampshire, imports it. They usually have it in stock. If you're a tallow freak, write them, and they'll see that you get some.

By the way, if you use silicones, or any other treatment in a volatile solvent base, be leery of applying it around the midsoles. Some glues are easily destroyed by certain solvents, and experimentation here can be terribly costly. If you're concerned about the edges of the midsoles, try good old fashioned shoe polish, which is just another wax dressing, and it is available in a neutral shade.

Moisture, per se, will not destroy boots if they are dried after use. "Drying" doesn't mean putting them on a radiator, flopping them into an oven, or toasting them on a stick over a fire. You can dry them over a fire in the field, if necessary, but if it's too hot for your hand, it's too hot for leather. Leather shrinks as it dries, and the shrinkage rate is a function of the drying rate. A boot dried too quickly, or at too high a temperature, can be badly damaged. The welt can shrink and pull out, or become so brittle that it cracks in use; the midsoles can curl dramatically; the uppers can grow brittle overnight. Dry boots slowly, at room temperatures with boot trees in them, and treat them after drying with a substance like Sno-Seal or Tierowa. A wet boot in the field is a true and majestic bummer, but dry socks (again!) will save the day.

A few more words on foot care are in order. Blisters do happen, often the evidence of carelessness from ill-fitting socks or loosely tied boots. If you sense a hot spot on your foot (usually on the heel), stop *immediately,* take off the boot and socks, and examine the area. If it's just reddening, dip into your friendly local first-aid bag and take out a piece of moleskin. Cut a hole in the moleskin a bit larger than the red spot, and put the sticky stuff in place, with the spot peeking out at you through the hole. This way, you've set a pad around the irritated spot so the boot can't get at it. If you were to simply cover the whole heel with moleskin, you'd still irritate the spot and later be forced to tear the tape off a real, live blister. A full-grown blister can be popped with a clean needle inserted deftly under one corner, either treated with an antiseptic or washed (I prefer the latter) and mole-skinned as above. Moleskin is handy stuff. You can get it at any drugstore. Trade names are many, but Dr. Scholl's Moleskin (dr. Mole's Schollskin??) or Dr. Scholl's Kiro-Felt come in convenient packages, and seem to be ubiquitous.

Beside moleskin, I carry a small box of, would you believe, Johnson & Johnson's Baby Powder. It's a luxury, like red wine, but it absorbs perspiration, reduces fric-tion, and feels good on my feet at the close of the day. The latter point is excuse enough for me. As I've said, quoting Old Nessmuk, "We don't go into the woods to rough it, we go to smooth it. We get it rough enough at home."

3. FROM THE SKIN OUT

"It ain't so much what you wear.
It's what you wear where."
—*Big Bill Broonzy*

In our sheltered world, the functional value of clothing is secondary to appearance. One of the appealing freedoms of backpacking is that it reverses the secular order of importance in many ways, and most of all in the appearance and quantity of your clothing. One of the penny-pinching joys of clothes for backpacking is that you have most of them lying around the house already. That is if they haven't been thrown out. Sure, there are several desirable specialty items you probably don't have, and there are some specialty items that work better than what you have already, but don't sweat it. You're outfitted, in all probability.

Clothing is basically uncomplicated. You should be protected from the sun, bugs, stray branches, and the rain. It should keep you warm in the cold. Most of the time, all you'll need is an old shirt or T-shirt and an old pair of loose, baggy, rumpsprung pants. If you're into wearing shorts, don't rush off and buy some cutesy-fartsy number labeled "hiking shorts." Find an old pair of pants and amputate.

Got a heavy shirt around the house? An old, smelly wool one that the dog sleeps on? Great. Maybe you have an old wool sweater. You're in business. All you need now is a cheapie vinyl poncho from your local Army–Navy store and you're set to go backpacking. We'll talk about the fancy gear later on, but don't be deterred from going because you're worried about being ill-clad or worried about not looking official. Don't laugh. Some people do worry about that. The inevitable result of a stringent workaday conformity we almost take for granted. If the haphazard look I happen to favor bugs you, go down to your friendly local work clothes emporium (or Sears, Wards, or J.C. Penney's if you're in suburbia) and get a polyester/cotton work shirt and work pants. Green's a good color. It fits with the surroundings, doesn't show the dirt for weeks, and is commonly worn. Avoid blue. According to the U.S. Army Quartermaster Corps, mosquitoes and black flies love it.

Let's begin inside your boots, and go through your normal items of clothing one at a time. Then we'll branch out into a discussion of how to keep warm and dry.

23

SOCKS

We went through this rap already in the chapter on boots, but it bears repeating. If you've bought new boots, they were undoubtedly fitted over two pairs of socks, one heavy and one light. This permits the outer sock to rub against the inner sock rather than your skin. The backpacker's choice has traditionally been wool, and for good reasons. Wool retains its air spaces and warmth when wet — and it will be wet sooner or later. Wool absorbs perspiration, and transfers some of it to the cuffs of the sock for evaporation. Wool is also resilient and provides a degree of cushioning for the feet.

I've worn a lot of different socks over the years, but I've pretty well settled on the Norwegian-made ragg sock as the sock for hard truckin'. For the past four years I've been wearing a stretch ragg called the North Cape. It wears like iron, washes well, and retains its shape and its bounce better than any sock I've ever used. There's another great virtue. My old lady and I can wear the same size in a stretch ragg, which greatly reduces the terrors of sorting socks that are one size apart.

Some people swear by the so-called "wick-dry" sock, a coarse sock, usually of orlon, nylon and cotton, with a nubbly, terrycloth-like inside that soaks up sweat and wicks it to the cuff where it can evaporate. Too many people have commented favorably on them for me to ignore, but I don't find them as comfortable as wool. Of the wick-dries that I've seen, and I think I've seen about all of them, I like the Esquire Thirsto the best. It's a Birdwick weave, which has been proven effective for some time now. Esquire seems to have done something to the cuffs to keep them from unraveling if you look at them. This is a common failing in wick-dry socks, by the way. The whole damn cuff sort of unwinds before your eyes.

For inner socks, I use either the North Cape or the Wigwam Mojave — both wool, both lightweight. The Wigwam fits better across the instep, but it's a bit more prone to shrinkage if you're careless. If you're allergic to wool or simply don't like the feel of it next to your skin, synthetic inner socks are readily available. Again, Wigwam makes a good one.

Carry extra socks for even an overnight, and at least three pairs for a long trip. Wash one set each day, and tie them on your pack to dry. This isn't the rattle of a deodorant-minded man. It's common sense! After a day's use, the socks are matted. They're less resilient, less absorptive, and don't fit as well. They're also soaked with salt, which is a dandy skin irritant. So change your socks, hear? And commit your feet to the agonizing joy of a cold stream.

CAMP FOOTGEAR

There are times when you arrive at a pleasant spot for setting up camp, yearning for something beside two and a half pounds of boot hanging from the end of each leg. A sturdy boot's great for walking, but the walking's over for the day. It's fine to traipse around the landscape barefoot; it feels wondrous free. But there's always some damn fool who's broken a beer bottle, or there's always a sharp rock or a rusty can half-buried. You can avoid these troubles with something simple like a pair of soleless moccasins or an old pair of low cut sneakers or a 49 cent pair of zoris from your local discount house.

I prefer moccasins. West Coasters opt for zoris. The economy-minded wear sneakers. The young, the brave, and the battle-scarred go barefoot. Take your choice. All I know is that it's a joy and a half to take off my boots after a long day, soak the canal boats in a stream, dry them lovingly, powder them, and treat them to dry socks and moccasins. Good soleless mocs are expensive. A good pair of elkhide mocs runs about eighteen bucks, and the ones with two layers of leather underfoot are over thirty. By the way, elkhide is not the hide of an elk. Elk leather is a leather trade term for a thick, specially tanned cowhide used for heavy duty applications. However, commercial buckskin is made of elk hides. Confused? So am I. No way in hell is Mrs. Roberts' little boy going to pay top dollar for moccasins. He went to Tandy's and bought a kit a few years ago for eight bucks. I presume the price is higher now, but it's still a saving and fun to put together.

PANTS

Wear what you have that's loose and baggy, and hope that some day somebody creates the ideal pants for the backpacker at a reasonable price. What's ideal? Well, my ideal pants would be light, tightly woven to repel wind and discourage insects, tough as nails, but soft enough that they won't chafe your hide, quick to dry, and free of belt loops. They'd also have one zippered pocket to secure essentials like car keys and knives. I'd prefer them low cut, but high-water pants are acceptable also. The main thing is to avoid having the hipbelt of the pack fall at the top of the pants. No hipbelt is engineered to fit over a belt, belt loops, and a heavy, interfaced double layer of fabric. All it will do is bite, pinch, roll and pummel your hide all day until you look like the plaintiff in a case of aggravated assault. Given the traditional state of pants design, all you can do is grin and bear it.

The closest I've seen to my ideal was the old Gerry climbing pants, long since discontinued and hellishly expensive. I cherish mine; when they're ready for the scrap heap, I'll cut them apart and pull a pattern from them. The lightweight orlon whipcord they're made of is a bit warm on a hot day, but other than that, it's well nigh perfect. Army surplus fatigues, especially the rip-stop cotton ones, are an excellent alternative. They're cheap, durable, loosely cut around the thighs, tightly woven, and quick drying. They lack the delicious feel of orlon whipcord, but they soften up after several washings, and get downright mellow in middle age. I like the kind with the cargo pockets, because I can carry trail munchies in them. Avoid the temptation to overload those big pockets, though. If you do, the pants are far less comfortable.

Whatever pants you decide to wear, try this simple test to see how they'll work on the trail. Put them on, and put one foot on a chair, as though you were planning to walk over it. If the pants bind in the crotch or bite into your upper thigh, or dig into the tender area behind your knees, they'll be bummers on the trail. Most pants, particularly jeans, are cut too snugly across the butt and in the thighs to be comfortable for trail walking. Apply the same test to cutoffs. You can, of course, loosen cut-offs by splitting the side seams a few inches. Bar tack the seam afterward, though, or you may wind up wearing an instant loincloth. That's no great hassle on the trail, but it's a barrel of chuckles for your friends when you walk into the Elm Tree Inn at Keene for a Purdyburger and a cold ale.

A few last words about pants. If you like to wear a belt you'll find that it interferes with the hipbelt on your packframe unless it's very soft and narrow. I've come up with two belts that do the job neatly. The first is simply a sleeping bag strap, a thin nylon web belt with a small friction buckle. The other is a little more elaborate. It's a piece of one inch tubular webbing that rock climbers use for swami belts and such, and two aluminum descending rings. All these things are available at your outfitter's. Run one end of the webbing through both rings and stitch it back to itself with heavy thread. Presto! A belt that's soft, strong and reasonably slip-proof.

UNDERWEAR AND OTHER UNMENTIONABLES

The fair-weather packer has three options: cotton, cotton or nylon net, or nothing at all. For men, it's easy. There isn't a great deal of synthetic underwear made for men if you eliminate the kind of stuff advertised in magazines with strange names like Lash & Leather and Modern Moresomes. The typical jockey shorts are cotton. They work. For women, whose undergarments are typically synthetic, it means going back to little girl underpants from Carter's or ripping off your old man's underwear (my wife's solution sometimes) or going without (her solution the rest of the time). At any rate, avoid nylon or rayon or whatnot materials because they breathe poorly and absorb moisture not a bit. After three days on the trail, you develop what feels like gangrene of the groin. Nylon's great in civilization, but in civilization you aren't walking uphill for twelve miles with twenty pounds on your back with only a small stream to luxuriate in at day's end.

I like nylon or polyester/cotton mesh underwear. It breathes, and dries in a flash. It's also cut lower than most underwear, which is a blessing when you're wearing a hipbelt. They're not easy to find, although some outfitters have them. Mine are labeled E*K*T, and they're Norwegian imports. They're worth the somewhat inflated price. As for the no-underwear concept, I'm not happy without underwear. Whether this is due to a Puritan upbringing or a well-founded fear of zippers I'm not certain, but I am certainly unhappy. If you dig it, do it.

Molly insists that I add three words about bras, to close this shocking section, so I will. They are these: ARE YOU KIDDING?

SHIRTS

I don't wear shirts except in cold weather or insanely buggy weather, preferring to walk barechested or covered by a fishnet shirt, which is nothing more than a bunch of holes held together by string. It doesn't cover much, but it fends off limbs fairly well, and it's excellent insulation, which I'll mention again later. Most people prefer a shirt, and almost anything you have around the house will do. I've worn a Lee polyester/cotton work shirt for five years for cool weather packing, and it's survived with honor. Any sturdy shirt will do. It should have long sleeves and pockets that button. Pockets with flaps are even better. Losing your compass because it fell out of your pocket when you were drinking out of a stream is a bummer — and I've found enough small items around stream crossings to prove that it happens with regularity.

Besides an outer shirt I'd wear a fishnet shirt under it. The fishnet ventilates well, and it doesn't absorb vast amounts of sweat and cling to your body like a wet horse blanket. Sure, it clings, but more like a very threadbare horse blanket. Fishnet shirts, particularly Duofold's polyester ones, dry quickly as well, which is an added benefit. And they're insulated. Wait a second, how can a bunch of holes be insulation? Easy. If that bunch of holes is covered with a lightweight, loose shirt open at the collar, it permits full circulation of air. Pull a sweater and a wind jacket over it, and cut the circulation to zilch, and you have a fairly thick blanket of warm, dead air. That's insulation, and much more effective insulation than a T-shirt.

RAINWEAR

If there's anything you can plan on in the East, it's adequate rainfall. No, it won't rain on your garden, and it won't rain in the river you want to paddle, but it will rain when it should snow, and it will rain the minute you plant your bootsoles on a trail.

Raingear poses a problem of sorts. With no raingear or poor raingear, you get soaked from the outside in. With good raingear, you get clammy from the inside out, because the coated fabric of the raingear doesn't permit your perspiration to evaporate. Neither option is exactly joy in the morning, but my experience indicates that you don't get nearly as wet from sweat as from rain, and on a chilly day, it's far more preferable to be warm and damp under good raingear than chilled to the bone and sopping wet. Let's look at your raingear options one by one, and keep in mind that your pack, waterproof or not, warrants its own raincoat, of which more later.

BARE SKIN

The human hide is a marvelous material, virtually unaffected by water. The most effective summer rainsuit imaginable for protection against a warm rain is a raincover on your pack and as little as law, conscience or trail traffic will permit on you. Nothing to dry out, nothing to shrink or stretch, nothing to stay clammy for hours, and very low cost. Ill suited to blackfly season, well-traveled trails or cold, or mixed group hiking.

PONCHOS

The standard item of raingear is a poncho, a surpassingly ugly device resembling a young bedsheet with a hole in the middle. The hole is usually, but not always, capped with a hood. This great, flapping thing drops over your dripping form, to be snapped together along its sides, thus effecting a measure of protection against windblown rain. At its best, a poncho is excellent head to knee protection. It can double as a tarp or a groundcloth, and because it's not exactly form-fitting, it permits plenty of air to circulate inside to counteract the clammies.

Plenty of room indeed when the wind is up and your poncho rises majestically over your ears and entwines lovingly around your pack. The copious folds of fabric reach out and put the snatch on every root and every branch from Bradley

Pond to the summit of Santanoni, and the long tail of the flapping orange beast is underfoot at every steep pitch. I concede the versatility and the effectiveness of the poncho — and if you find me wearing one, you'll know that some search and rescue group has wrapped my dead body in it! I've worn 'em, but the twin vices of flapping and snagging united one day on a horrendous bushwhack along an open ridge to dampen my enthusiasm forever. And that was a good poncho, maybe the best available at the time. Coated 1.9 ounce ripstop nylon; generous hood with a zippered gusset at the wishbone to ventilate with in a mile rain; big, meaty snaps set in reinforcing tabs; grommets at each corner; an extra length of fabric in the rear that could be unsnapped and dropped to cover a man wearing a pack; all seams felled and hand-sealed to boot. A prime garment. If you like ponchos, that's the kind to get, for sure.

The distinctions between a cheapie poncho and a good one are easy to spot. The best ponchos are hemmed around the edges, and snaps and grommets are set into the doubled layer of fabric and reinforced as well, usually with pack fabric but sometimes with leather. The cheapie is rarely hemmed along the long side. It's cut out of a 54 or 60 inch fabric and the finished edges of the cloth (the selvage edges) hang out in the breezes. The snaps are set in this single layer of cloth, and aren't distinguished by their permanence. The good poncho is made with felled seams that are sealed with a goop that has the smell and texture of model airplane cement, while the cheapie is joined with a simple unfinished seam that isn't sealed. Felled seams cost money; so does hand sealing. Don't expect fancy finished details on low-priced gear. Oddly enough, a cheapie poncho may be made of a perfectly acceptable fabric. So, if you're willing and able to do some sewing, you can turn one of them into a very fine garment. Be apprised, though, that the fabric most used in the low-cost poncho is not a fancy coated ripstop. It's a heavier rubberized nylon that's far less fragile and far more bombproof over the years.

For the first-time packer, the super cheap vinyl poncho is fine. You're not going to be off the trail anyway, so the lack of durability isn't a factor.

RAIN JACKETS

I like rain jackets; at least some of them. A good rain jacket is a versatile garment. It sheds water well; it's a useful windbreaker, and it can be worn around town where you wouldn't be caught dead wearing a poncho. Rain jackets come in three basic types. Simplest and cheapest is the single layer coated nylon jacket with a hood. Another common type is the heavy mountain parka made of an outer layer of coated nylon with an inner layer of polyester/cotton to absorb perspiration. A third type is a double shell garment made of two layers of coated nylon. The cheapest type works well if it's finished well. If there are no seams across the top of the shoulders, the jacket is long enough to cover your backside, and the seams are felled, there's no reason why the single shell won't shed rain. In time, however, the coating will wear and the jacket will leak, but you don't have a lot of dollars invested either. You'll sweat in any rain jacket. If you can find a single shell with a means of ventilating under the arms (mesh panel preferred, grommets a poor second) and a gusseted cuff that you can loosen, you'll be a lot more comfortable. A two-way zipper on a single shell garment well nigh approaches paradise.

DRY HIKER ⅗ DRY PIPE

The waterproof mountain parkas are generally better sewn than the single shells. The seams are felled, the hoods are more generous, and the lining adds a degree of comfort. Yet they're still a single layer jacket as far as long-term water repellency goes. The addition of a second layer of fabric — any fabric — will increase water repellency by an order of magnitude, but my experience has been that even these big coats will leak in time.

My own favorite in the raingear derby is an oddball jacket that's been around for a long time, the Gerry All Weather parka. I generally try to avoid specific endorsements of gear. That isn't the purpose of this book. But having walked six thousand feet of descent on Rainier in a heavy rain driven by high winds on a forty degree day and arrived at Paradise Inn bone dry from the hips up, and having walked three days on the Northville-Lake Placid Trail in a steady, heavy downpour bone dry from the hips up, I'm forced to conclude that the All Weather is one helluva coat.

This long jacket is made of coated nylon, with another layer of coated nylon as a liner from the waist up. The inner lining extends to the elbows. It has a very full double layered hood, the cuffs are gusseted and closed with big Velcro tabs, and the back is ventilated by a big mesh panel covered with a flap. The panel doesn't do a thing for you when you're wearing a pack but it's fine around camp. Strange to say, a two-way zipper is lacking. It's a sweaty beast on a warm day, but I don't find it as cloying as a single shell.

CAGOULES

A cagoule is a maxidress with a hood, exquisitely tailored in coated nylon. It's lined above the waist, and features a kicky big pocket across the chest. Actually, the garment is designed to protect a mountaineer perched on a tiny ledge three thousand feet above nothing. It's a pullover garment, which is well sealed except for a short zipper, usually gusseted, at the throat. A cagoule is long enough to draw your feet up into when you're sitting. It's also sufficiently roomy to wear over a big down parka. A good cagoule will stop rain, snow, sleet and wind with ease. You don't see many of them on the trail because they're relatively expensive, generally in short supply, and pretty much unknown to the average backpacker. Those who wear them, and my wife is one, love them with an unholy passion best reserved for animate objects.

A cagoule isn't a garment you have to poke at and inspect meticulously to find a good one. They're a specialty item made by a few people for a few people who plan to go in harm's way, and they're uniformly high in quality, with felled seams and the best procurable fabric. They're worth looking at if total protection is what you're after and you're willing to sacrifice some versatility and a lot of breath-ability for it.

RAIN PANTS AND CHAPS

All the above garments will expose some part of your legs to the rain, although a cagoule will come to below your knees and a poncho to about your knees. Addi-

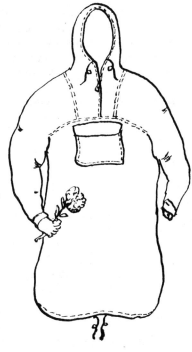

CAGOULE

tional rain protection is useful. Probably the cheapest, lightest and most comfortable kind is afforded by rain chaps, which are pantlegs made of coated nylon that attach to your belt by cords. Nothing fancy, but all you need. Rain jacket wearers, on the other hand, need rather more to keep totally dry. The answer here is a pair of rain pants, pajama-like bags of coated nylon that make you look like a refugee from Chairman Mao's long march.

The main thing to be concerned about is not the fanciness of the needlework, but whether the things can be put on over your boots. There are few things in life as joyless as taking off your boots in the midst of a downpour to put on your raingear. Chaps are usually fat in the legs, so they'll accommodate a boot. Pants may be bummers. Mine have short zippers at the cuff to snug them down after you put them on, and I find this a desirable feature, particularly when walking in cripplebush. Some rain pants are made with snaps or Velcro tabs to effect the same end, but the zipper arrangement, while possibly more fragile, is neater and leaves less material flopping around to hang up when you don't want it to.

It doesn't have to be raining to make chaps or rain pants useful. You can get completely soaked walking through a dewy field or through the puckerbush right after a rain, too, and that inviting stump at camp is wet for three days after a shower. I use my rain pants a lot. Molly, being a cagoule wearer, carries chaps, which are less useful as loungearounds on soggy ground. Her motto, though, seems to be "Happiness is a warm, dry backside", so she carries a scrap of quarter-inch thick Ensolite that's about a foot square. It's a holdover from her Girl Scout days, when they made little embroidered oilcloth squares that were called "sit-upons". I laugh the thing to scorn — and shamelessly steal it from her the second she gets off it!

WARMWEAR FROM THE CLOSET

The summer packer doesn't face the obvious problems of keeping warm that the winter freak must, but a fifty degree night with only a torn T-shirt for protection isn't the epitome of comfort. Chances are that you already have a bulky wool sweater or a heavy wool shirt, either of which will do the job admirably. I stress wool because it retains its air spaces, and thence its warmth, when wet. If you're one of those unfortunates who's allergic to wool, orlon's the next best — and indeed the only — choice. If you have several sweaters from which to choose, I'd recommend a turtleneck as first choice and a crew neck next. You lose too much warmth with a V-neck.

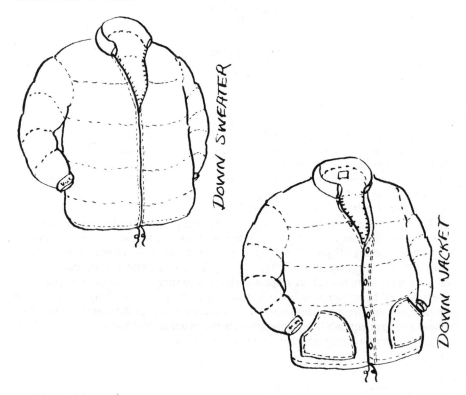

DOWN JACKETS

Since sweaters and shirts are bulky and heavy, you might want to consider some alternatives that are lighter and more compact. The obvious one is a down jacket. It needn't be a thick, overlapping tube coat designed for a quick jog up McKinley. That's overkill of the rankest sort. What you want is a simple, straightforward hip-length jacket of sewn-through (quilted) construction. It should have an insulated standup collar. While I like a jacket that can be closed with either snaps or a zipper, and has a draft flap covering the zipper, the so-called "down sweater", which has only a zipper, is certainly adequate. A typical jacket will weigh about a pound and a half and is filled with about a half pound of down. The sweater will usually weigh a bit less. Either will stuff easily into a quart beer bottle minus the neck, and will be warm over just a T-shirt at about twenty degrees. They're useful knock-around jackets in winter, too, so you're not laying out your cash for something that's doomed to live in your pack most of the time.

There are a few things you should check out when you look for a lightweight downie, and a few things you can afford to ignore, like ripstop nylon. Sure, I know that everybody and his hiking friend will fill your head with the wonders of ripstop, and I can't quibble with its usefulness, But I can't quibble with good old downproof 2.2 ounce nylon taffeta either. I've used a taffeta downie, a Sierra Designs Sierra Jacket, for seven years now, winter and summer, and the only holes in it were put there by my own carelessness with fire. Construction details are far more important than shell material in a jacket. So is the fit of the coat, which should be loose without being sloppy, and relatively snug around the neck to cut down heat losses. The coat should have a drawstring at either the waist or the draw-hem to seal it against wind losses, and the cuffs should be elasticized and set with snaps so they can be worn loosely or snugly as you desire.

I like a dual closure system — a zipper and a draft flap over it that closes with snaps. I'm delighted if the zipper is sewn on with two rows of stitches, and back-stitched or boxed or locked securely in some other way at both ends. A two-way zipper isn't essential on a short jacket, so don't worry about that point. A coil zipper is plenty strong, but I tend to like the old #5 YKK molded Delrin zipper for jackets because I'm accustomed to it. I also like the Talon ladder coil. Both are easier to engage than most coils. Don't take that as gospel, though. Try for yourself.

A sewn-through jacket isn't a terribly sophisticated garment, but there are still ways in which you can tell the good ones without a scorecard. It should be moderately plump. If you were to put the jacket on a flat surface and lay a piece of cardboard on it, it should be about three inches thick, and the tubes should be well filled. There's an easy way to check this. Hold the jacket up to the light and you can see the down filling in each tube as though it was on X-ray film. The tube won't be absolutely filled; the sewn-through method precludes that. The region around where the inner and outer shells are sewn together is too snug to admit any meaningful amount of down, and there will always be a holiday showing. A bummer will be only partly filled. Don't write it off immediately, though. Pat the down around to distribute it evenly and look again. You may be surprised. Chances are that you won't, though, because if there's enough down to really fill a tube, there isn't much room for the stuff to wander in.

Pleased with the jacket? Great. Check out the one you're going to take home with you in the same way. There's a good reason for this. A sewn-through jacket is made by stuffing the body pieces and the sleeves (opened flat, of course) with a measured amount of down, distributing it evenly throughout the piece, and stitching the tubes with the down already in place.

You might well check out a few other things. Are the snaps set well, or do they look like they'll tear out with a small tug? All solid? Groovy. The zipper works smoothly? The drawstring around the waist or the hips works? Fine. That's rarely a problem, but occasionally somebody sews the cord into the drawhem in a few places by mistake. No loose stitches or badly tensioned ones that could snag and tear out? Fine. How about the side seams, especially the ones inside the jacket? I like to see a finished seam with a cap on it (a taped seam, if you will). This seam is usually caught pretty closely. Fabric is money, and you don't waste money by cutting huge seam allowances. Just make sure that the seam is caught all the way down, and not laying open at any point. Follow it right down the sleeve while you're at it, because this seam is finished (taped or surged) after the jacket is assembled. Okay? Dandy. Got the stuff bag with it? It's in the pocket of the jacket. Fine. Pay the man and go home smiling.

DOWN VESTS

A down vest is a sewn-through jacket without sleeves — a most useful, superlight commodity for the three-season walker. It's not as useful a go-to-the-store garment as a jacket, perhaps, but a vest under a windshell is very warm indeed. Most vests have a single method of closing, either snaps or a zipper. Of the two, I prefer snaps. They may be less efficient, but a failed zipper is failed indeed, and a failed snap leaves six more of the little sweeties to get the job done.

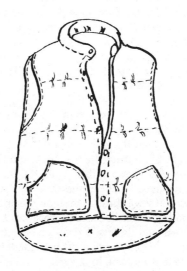

DOWN VEST

I don't use a vest. Molly does, particularly on day trips. She still favors a jacket for a longer trip, though. However, both of us wear vests almost constantly in the winter. No, not afield. In this great ark of a farmhouse of ours. Don't laugh! Fuel oil's approaching forty cents a gallon, and it ain't a'gonna get any cheaper. I'm beginning to view a down vest as a useful commodity for winter mountaineering in my dining room!

A vest, of course, can be evaluated the same way a jacket can be, with one exception. I like a vest that has a little flap on the back that hangs down over the kidneys. Cozier, somehow. It may be all in my head, but I think not. Try both styles, and make up your mind. It's your vest, after all.

GOOD GOOSE, DOWNRIGHT DUCK   1891323

If you're a catalog reader, you may be curious as to why I haven't differentiated between goose down and duck down fill in a jacket or vest. In the first place, the loft of a sewn-through jacket is severely inhibited by the nature of the tubes. There's only so much down you can cram into a sewn-through tube without arriving at a point where you're buying nothing in terms of insulation, and there's only a limited volume in which the down can expand as well. That being the case, the slight difference in loft between good goose and downright duck isn't significant. Of course, nothing's free. If one jacket is priced considerably lower than another, and it isn't on sale, and finish details are comparable, somebody's cutting down on either the quantity or the quality of the fill — or both. I wouldn't sweat this if the garment comes from a maker of known reputation. If you're a catalog reader, you know the names. Gerry, North Face, Sierra Designs, Camp 7, Class 5, and Alpine Designs are so well known in the trade that you shouldn't have to worry about being burned by their gear. Eastern Mountain Sports, Eddie Bauer and Holubar Mountaineering are catalog houses that make their own stuff, and it's first rate. Recreational Equipment builds their own gear, too, and it's good. And there are some small manufacturers who do nice things. Mountain Products is one. So is Thaw. So is Down East. And there's another name you don't associate with down, I'll bet. Woolrich. Downrich?? No, Woolrich, believe it or not. If you're buying from a catalog, you can only trust the catalog outfitter and the maker. If you're buying from a shop, all you can trust is your local outfitter — and the maker. The outfitter stands behind his gear, to be sure, but the manufacturer is the guy who has to have his act together.

POLYESTER — THE HYDROCARBON HONKER

When you're off at your outfitter's grokking down jackets, you might do yourself a favor and take a look at the polyester-filled garments. They're a bit bulkier per unit of thickness, as they don't compress quite as well, and a bit heavier per unit thickness as well. They're also about forty percent cheaper for comparable warmth, and they need no special care and feeding. They also absorb zilch moisture, and even if you fall in the nearest rushing brook, they can be wrung dry, shaken a few times for effect, and put on again. I'm a down freak, but Polarguard and Fiberfill II impress me greatly for three-season backpacking.

I've long held the notion, by the way, that insulation thickness may be the most critical parameter in determining the warmth of a jacket, but insulation density's also right up there in importance. We've always defined insulation as a thickness of dead air, and it's certainly a valid definition. However, I've been straying away from the gospel a bit and entertaining a notion that maybe the synthetics, which are surely denser, permit less circulation of air and furthermore resist wind penetration better than down. It just may be, when all the tests are in, that an inch of Polarguard® is a more effective insulator than an inch of down. I have only empirical evidence gathered from using a lot of Polarguard stuff and some Fiberfill II stuff. The same density that inhibits air circulation and makes the synthetics "warm" also will entrap body moisture in a very cold environment and freeze it, rather than permit it to pass through and dissipate to the atmosphere or crystallize on the outer shell of the garment. This won't inhibit the loft of the garment a bit, but it sure as hell isn't going to be pleasant. Until we all know more, I'm going to praise Polarguard and Fiberfill II to the skies for three-season use, and reserve judgment on them for extreme cold.

WINDGEAR

Wind cools you off; it cools you very quickly and unpleasantly when you're wet. In fact, if you're soaked to the skin in a very exposed location where you can't find shelter, you could wind up very dead indeed with the air temperature well above freezing. The phenomenon is called hypothermia, and we'll talk about it in more detail later. I bring it up here to let you know that protection from wind can be critical. It isn't often that dramatic, but why even be uncomfortable if you can avoid it with a little thought?

WIND SHIRT

I don't carry an honest-to-god wind jacket except in winter or on big, exposed mountains anytime. Yes, Virginia, Mt. Washington is winter – anytime! I do carry a rain parka, and Old Blue serves me well for the breezy moments of a summer summit. But Old Blue's two layers of coated nylon. While it's impervious to rain and wind, it's also impervious to sweat. In brief, it's hot as hell, and in cold weather, your clothing can get dangerously sodden. You need wind protection that will transmit your body's moisture to the air, and at the same time keep the winds of spring from roaring through.

The summer packer usually finds that his sturdy work shirt is sufficient for most of his needs, but there are times when a lightweight nylon shell is a very desirable garment. If you can stand the materials, which look like draperies for a Moroccan bagnio, truck on down to your local downhill ski shop at season's end and pick up a wind shirt, which is simply a dense nylon shirt with snap buttons. They work, they're cheap, and they're light. A better choice is a hip-length nylon parka with a hood and a zipper closure, but a good one isn't cheap and a cheap one isn't good. Let's take a look at a good one – the Windstopper, by Sierra West, a small shop in Santa Barbara. We can go to school on the Windstopper, which isn't widely distributed, and use it as a criterion against which you can place any shell you find.

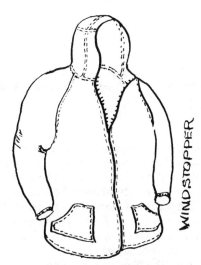

The Windstopper's made of a very high count nylon taffeta. I haven't counted the threads, but I'd guess about 160 warp by 120 fill – and that's a very dense nylon, particularly considering good taffeta is 160 by 90. It's so dense, in fact, that it feels almost crinkly. You're not going to count threads per inch in a shop, but you can try to suck air through the fabric. You can barely suck air through a Windstopper. This isn't a coated fabric; you don't want that for wind protection generally. However, it's almost as impermeable to air. If you can suck air through the jacket you're looking at with ease, the wind can go through it just as easily. I know of no surer test for a wind shell than that.

Next, check out the detail work, because that's what keeps the jacket together through years of hard usage. How are the seams sewn? Are they felled, like a Windstopper's, or left unfinished? An unfinished seam in nylon will unravel with a harsh glance. A surged seam is better, but rather crude.

Is the zipper sewn in well, or just hung in place with a lick and a promise and a single row of stitches? It should be sewn with a double row through a doubled, finished layer of fabric.

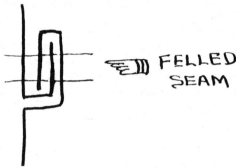

FELLED SEAM

There are cheaper and simpler ways, one of which is half-baked but acceptable, and one which is pretty poor.

UNFINISHED SEAM

A windbreaker should have a drawhem so you can snug it up if you need to. Some folks like the draw cord at the waist, which permits unimpeded thigh movement. Others like it at the bottom of the jacket, to keep the chilly breezes from their backsides. Are the ends of the drawhem (where the cord peeks through) finished, or do you find a raw edge of fabric there to unravel? By the way, I'm all thumbs. I like a fairly wide drawhem so I can go fishing for the end of the cord that I inevitably lose. A narrow drawhem concentrates abrasion in the same area, and all nylon is prone to damage by abrasion.

Now check out the hood. The Windstopper's hood is a complex one, cut out of six pieces, including a generous facing. The zipper actually ends at around your mouth, which is a terror if you wear a beard, but it provides a generous tunnel for face protection and a snug, draft-free closure around the neck. A jacket hood that ends at your ears is groovy in a ten-mile wind on an eighty degree day, but it's an eighteen carat pain in the cheeks in a rear blow. The Windstopper's hood is the real thing.

The hood's drawcords should exit through grommets, otherwise the material will fray. This isn't too critical on a crummy hood, because you can't draw the damn thing closed without strangling anyway.

The cut of the garment should be generous. It should fit easily over a sweater or wool shirt or down jacket if that's what you'll be wearing. Raglan sleeves with generous scyes (a fancy word for armholes) are imperative unless you get off on living in a straight-jacket. This is where the cheap jackets fall on their zippers, because this takes a lot of fabric, and fabric is money. Actually, it doesn't look like it should take that much more fabric, but a well-cut, generous shoulder and sleeve requires some rakish curves, and this means a generous pile of scrap in even the most organized cutting rooms. How to tell if it's roomy enough? Try it on over a down jacket or a heavy sweater! How better to tell?

One more thing. Does the jacket you're looking at cover your peaked little behind, or does it leave you hanging out and shivering? It covers you? Good. You'll appreciate that. If these things tally up right, the jacket you're looking at compares with the Windstopper, which means it's a fine windshell. You can buy it with some assurance that you're not getting ripped off.

There's another breed of wind jacket you should know about, and that's what's come to be known as the 60/40 parka. A mountaineer's coat — a big, heavy, bombproof job with an outer shell of nylon/cotton or polyester/cotton, an inner shell usually of nylon, four big bellows pockets closed with Velcro tabs, a back pocket, and an expedition-type tunnel hood. It's become sort of a uniform for the "serious" hiker.

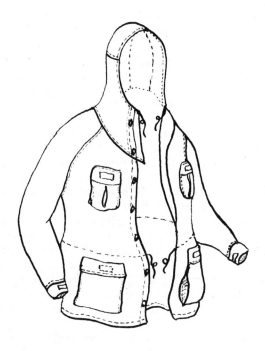

DOUBLE SHELL
MOUNTAIN PARKA

And not without reason. These big coats are tough, absolutely windproof, moderately water repellent, comfortable, and as practical around town as on the trail. They are a great luxury, but not a necessity. My advice to you is to save up for something you really need, but it seems inevitable that you'll cast calf eyes on a 60/40 sooner or later; so you might as well know something about the nature of the beast.

There might be discussion about the origin of the design, but there isn't any about the origin of the name or the development of the 60/40's final form. The name comes from a type of fabric, 60 percent cotton and 40 percent nylon, in which the nylon is the warp and the cotton the fill. The design came from Sierra Designs, one of the hotbeds of creativity in the backpacking revolution. Their jacket was, and is, called, simply enough, the 60/40 parka. It's spawned a host of imitations, all of them pretty fine coats, from all the major equipment builders. A discrete blend of polyester and cotton (the polyester filaments and the cotton are twisted together into a single tough thread) seems to be the favored material, and linings range from nylon taffeta to a lightweight, nubbly polyester/cotton. Names range from the prosaic, with Mountain Parka being a favorite, to the lofty. You know the kind. Pick a mountain, any mountain, as long as it's a big mother mountain, and hang the name on your gear. (As a casual aside, there is a small peak around Rainier called Mother Mountain, but nobody's used it. Mother Mountain Parka! How about that, ad fans!) No matter what the parka is dubbed, it somehow winds up being called a 60/40, which must be a mixed blessing at best for Sierra Designs and an unmitigated horror for everybody else.

This style of parka seems to bring out the best in a manufacturer. I've looked at 60/40's made by Holubar, Alpine Designs, Class Five, North Face, Down East, Farwest and Trails West, and they're all good value. They're cut generously and sewn well. The zippers are big and have a good feel. The snaps are sturdy, and the draft flaps are wide. The hoods fit well, the pockets are big and strongly sewn in place, and nobody skimps on the Velcro. And Sierra Designs chugs along with their original fabric, fully lines their coat in a Ventile-type cotton, finishes their overweight moose with the loving attention to detail that Ferrari's racing mechanics devote to crankshafts, charges a huge sum for it in comparison with everybody else, and simply can't make enough of them.

Sure, I could nitpick little details that make the difference in cost and overall appearance, but most of them don't matter in terms of overall functionality. The 60/40's pockets are a little bit deeper. The jacket is cut a little fuller around the arms, shoulders and back. The zipper's heavier than it needs to be. The lining extends out onto the draft flap and there's a second interior draft flap from the wishbone on up. The Velcro tabs on the cuffs and pockets are a bit bigger, and the cuff gusset is larger. The lining is full-length, and done in a very costly fabric. You don't need any of these unless you're really into winter hiking. They're overdesigned for summer use in the East, and the 60/40 is the most overdesigned of the lot.

Nevertheless, they're fine looking coats, with a tough, official air about them, and sooner or later you'll fall for one. You won't take it backpacking with you unless the weather's truly lousy, but you'll wear the damn thing 150 days a year. And what does this all prove? Nothing much, really, except that there's a certain go-to-hell joy about owning something that's a little bit better than it needs to be. Or, with deference to the 60/40 that hangs on my wall, a whole lot better than it needs to be.

HYPOTHERMIA AND OTHER NASTY THINGS

If this is a book about three-season backpacking, why am I chattering so much about insulation and rain and wind protection? Just that our summers get interrupted regularly by intimations of autumn, and our springs and falls are mostly winter, to folks from other parts of the country. In short, it can be right nippy in the mountains, and storm fronts are persistent and long lived. Further, the higher elevations (anything above 4000 feet) are essentially subarctic terrain. More than one luckless hiker out for a romp in the Adirondacks has suffered from exposure in August, and the Presidential Range in the White Mountains has killed off more unwary walkers than any range in North America. The Northeastern mountains aren't big by Western standards, but they can brew up, on short notice, some of the most vicious weather this side of Donali Pass on McKinley.

I've seen a balmy seventy degree August afternoon in the Adirondacks turn completely around in two hours to a thirty degree day with high winds and driving rain that turned to snow. One night the mercury in my thermometer wailed once and dropped out of sight — nineteen above and damp, with rain and snow still falling. Molly and I were dry in our bulletproof raingear, and warm in our downies at Uphill Leanto, where we ate in comfort and prepared dinners and hot tea for badly chilled hikers who sought the leanto's shelter, teeth a-chattering and hands too chilled to light a match. We hiked the next day under leaden skies and a brisk wind in comfort, although I concede that a pair of gloves would have been pleasant. The wind rose that night and the thermometer stayed low as a high pressure ridge blew through. The next morning the clouds had vanished, and the sky was an achingly clear, deep blue. It was the most perfect day I've ever seen on an Eastern mountain — and we were all alone to enjoy it. Everybody else had packed up and left because they were unprepared for this dramatic weather shift.

The physiological mechanism to watch out for here is called hypothermia. Simply translated, it means loss of heat. The news media people call it exposure, as in "died of exposure". It works like this. Your body is happy at a normal temperature of 98.6 degrees. In cold weather, or in a high heat loss situation like wet clothing and high wind, your body will attempt to maintain this normal temperature. The first step is reduction of blood flow to the extremities by closing down little throttling valves in the capillaries. This phenomenon explains why frostbite strikes first at the fingers and toes. There is no mechanism for vasoconstriction in the head and trunk. The body will, in a sense, sacrifice its extremities to maintain its vital functions. In time, even shutting down the extremities may not work. The body temperature continues to fall. At about 95 degrees, shivering begins — an attempt on the body's part to generate a little more heat. Below 95, the shivering becomes almost uncontrollable. Your extremities are numb and your speech becomes slurred. A bit lower and shivering stops. Your muscles stiffen, and you may even feel warmer. When your body temperature drops below 90, you're in grave trouble. Your thought processes are messed up and you move stumblingly. Below 85, you become irrational, lapsing into unconsciousness at around 80. After that, you die.

If this sounds grim, it's intended to. A wet hiker on a fifty-degree day who's overtaken by high winds (not unusual after a rain) is in big, big trouble if he has no way of conserving his body's heat. Prolonged exposure can worsen the situation dramatically because the hiker's mobility and judgment are impaired. This should not be a problem for the three-season hiker who has reasonable protection against wind, rain, and cold in his pack, enough food to keep the internal fires burning, and sense enough to avoid an autumn traverse of the Presidentials until he's fully aware of the potential hazards.

A QUICK WARM TRICK OR THREE

Late September maybe. Early May, maybe. Maybe even good old July. But it's cold outside. Not cold that poses a danger, but cold that sneaks in around the edges when you're not looking. You don't have a downie, but you do have raingear, a shirt and a heavy, loosely woven sweater. Off with the shirt and on with the sweater. Then put on the shirt. This keeps the wind from penetrating the loose weave of the sweater and buys you some warmth. No wind, you say? That's rare. You don't notice a two mile per hour wind drift. It barely deflects smoke from your pipe. But your body's temperature control mechanism feels it. Still a bit chilly? Put on your rainwear, hood and all. It'll help.

Feet cold? Put a hat on, an old Navy watch cap or a light wool job favored by cross-country skiers. Remember, the flow of blood to your scalp and head never throttles down. At 40 degrees, a third of your heat losses are through your scalp. If the hat doesn't do it, and it may not if your boots have been soaked, remove your boots and your wet socks, and reach into your pack for a polybag. Most backpackers carry a few extra for repackaging or storing trash. Some people routinely double bag stuff like oatmeal. At any rate, it costs next to zilch in weight to carry a few extra polybags. Pull a polybag over your bare feet, and slip on your dry socks over it. Then put on your boots. Wow! Instant warm feet. It's the old vapor barrier principle familiar to Eastern backpackers, readers of Jack Stephenson's Warm-Lite catalog, and Bob Wood's column in *Wilderness Camping.*

A cautionary note must be added here. The baggie trick is a cold weather trick. Extensive use of it in moderate weather can cause a persistent skin fungus infection. This, however, shouldn't preclude its use around camp if your feet are chilly.

Hands a bit chilly? Use your socks for mittens. Ah, but your dry ones are on your feet already, and you read what I said about wet clothing. Back to the baggies. Pull the socks on your paws and pull a baggie OVER them.

A bit chilly at bedtime? Keep the hat on, even in a mummy bag. Keep the dry stocks on, as well. You'll shed them soon enough, but they'll help to get your body on the line.

None of these tricks are cure-alls. No amount of clothing, of whatever kind, will make you warm if you're not generating some heat of your own. The simplest way is to eat something, and wash it down with a hot, sweet drink.

4. PICKIN' YOUR PACK

Irate mother of Boy Scout to HNR:
"That packframe wasn't abused. It
just broke."
Boy Scout to HNR:
"Yeah, it wasn't a very big limb I
was chopping with it."

The optimum way to transport your gear into the wild green yonder is to have somebody else do it for you. Unfortunately, this requires either a whole lot of riches or a very dedicated, very strong lover. My wife is intensely liberated until marching time rolls around, at which point she willingly abets any chauvinistic tendencies I have. And if I could afford bearers and a cushioned palanquin, do you think I'd be writing this book? No way! I'd be out there in the boonies truckin' along in style!

It's a safe guess to assume that your situation doesn't differ too widely from mine; so chances are you'll need to acquire something in which to stuff your stuff. The choice of most backpackers is the frame pack, a jobbie that looks like a small aluminum ladder with a packbag fastened to it. They come in various exotic configurations, and to describe each and every one of them would be overkill. What you do need to know is how a packframe works, how it's put together, and how you can pick one out that will do the job for you.

43

In essence, a packframe is a ladder with shoulder straps and a waistband to attach to your body. At its best, it can ease the task of carrying a load, but it can never remove the burden from you. At its worst, it can be an instrument of torture that seemingly magnifies the load, and bites you at every step. The theory behind the packframe is pretty straightforward. We're imperfectly adapted to walking on two legs because we still have the long and relatively wobbly torso of a primate.

Ideally, we carry heavy loads best on the top of our head, where our spine is in compression, and it's strongest. The load is transmitted neatly to our pelvis girdle and thence to our thighs and buttocks, our strongest muscle groups. You've all seen pictures of some stringy, undernourished Indian dock walloper toting 500 pound cartons on his head. He's evolved the most efficient mode of carrying the load — but it's still a damn tough way to make a living! And carrying something on the top of your head is efficient only as long as the terrain is level, the footing secure, and the underbrush buried in concrete. On the trail, it's a bit more chancy.

But a few brilliant souls, whose names are lost in antiquity, reasoned that man can carry heavy burdens in a sack fitted closely to his back. The closer it fitted, the easier to carry. Someone else figured out that you could transfer the load more directly to your legs if you put a headstrap — called a tumpline — on the pack, ran it high across your forehead up into the hairline, which relieved some weight from your shoulders. This enabled some of my *Habitant* ancestors to tote prodigious loads across portages in the days of the fur trade. Here's some 120-pound dude sashaying across Grand Portage with 270 pounds on his back — and this is just a pleasant break in the day's routine of fourteen hours of paddling. The tumpline works, after a fashion, but you'd best be pretty cordy to begin with or it can simply destroy you.

Later on, some people decided that a rigid frame, with or without a tumpline, was the only way to go. The load was kept all in one piece without eating great holes in your spine. But it still took a moose to do it easily. Sometime after World War II, Dick Kelty figured out that if you took a ladder frame, contoured it to fit the body, added a belt, cinched the belt up snugly around your middle, and let the weight of the burden fall on your hips, life became a lot easier. So much easier, in fact, a whole new industry was spawned. Dick Kelty now tools around the blue Pacific on his very own sailboat. The secret was out.

KELTY STANDARD PACKFRAME

Now count the array of packframes on the market — and these are just the better-known lines! Kelty, Camp Trails, Alpine Designs, Jan Sport, Gerry, Universal Field Equipment, Mountain Equipment, Alpenlite, Adventure-16 and Sunbird. There are more every day, to include a rash of cutely-named imports which up to now have been garbage. But there was a time when we all laughed at Japanese cameras and electronics gear, too.

Any of the better-known brands will do the job for years, as well as the offbeat ones. This is still a business that people get into because they honestly feel they can do it better. Back to the basic rule of all equipment selection — find a piece of gear that *you* can live with comfortably! "Comfortably" is important. You live with a packframe on the trail. It's snuggled up to you for 8 to 12 hours, and an improperly fitting frame can be an instrument of torture. Don't feel that you have to buy a certain brand because your buddies have told you it's good, or a magazine has told you it's good, or an outfitter tells you that he used it, or that Joe Hero-climber uses it.

Try the pack on. Have it fitted to you by a knowledgeable outfitter, and ask him to load the animal with a good weekend's weight of gear — say about a fifth of your body weight. Walk around. Go up and down stairs. Take it off and put it back on a few times. Do the shoulder straps adjust quickly and stay adjusted? Does the hip belt do the same? How about a quick release? Does the pack sway from side to side or hang in there solidly? Does it bite you on the hips, or chafe your back, or dig into your trapezius muscles? Does it want to pull you over backward? Sometimes just a little adjusting is necessary. Everybody's bod has a unique configuration, and any widely-sold pack can be tinkered to fit most people reasonably well. Some things, like the ease of operation of a hipbelt buckle, can't be. Take your time. A lot of money is on the line. No outfitter worth his salt will rush you.

After you've found a packframe, or maybe several different packframes, that fit you pretty well, be sure to check out construction details. Most packframes are made of aluminum tubing, usually 6061-T6. The first digit identifies the alloy type, in this case magnesium and silicon. The second digit tells whether or not it has been modified since its original development. In this case, it hasn't. The last two digits either identify the aluminum purity or, in the case of 6061, the old designation numbers. The "T" suffix is an indicator of temper, which is one of the major factors governing strength, hardness and ductility. In this case, "T" indicates a heat-treated alloy, and the "6" tells you that it's been solution heat treated and artifically aged to stability. 6061-T6 is not the strongest aluminum alloy available and not the easiest to weld. However, high strength combines with good fatigue resistance and a high degree of weldability to produce the standard packframe alloy. Other alloys may work as well or even better in a non-welded configuration. The point here is simple. If the frame has held up in use for others, it'll probably hold up for you.

Avoid all rolled and welded tube on principle, though; you'll occasionally run across this in cheap frames. I'd also like to counsel you to avoid magnesium frames. Mag is superlight, there's no doubt of that, but mag is terribly difficult to fabricate at a reasonable price. Furthermore, magnesium rusts and is not as strong as the standard aluminums.

Now that you've found a comfortable frame constructed of an alloy proven in use, consider some refinements of construction details.

In general, packframes are either welded or assembled. The welded frame (Kelty, for example) is a rigid unit that will deflect precious little if you stand it on one corner and push down on the other. The assembled frame (Jan Sport and Alpine Designs, for examples) has side rails like the welded frame, but the crossmembers are fitted to the siderails by some sort of sophisticated T-fitting which is pinned or bolted in place. Joe and Mary mountaineer typically despise this construction method, because they say it isn't as strong as the welded unit. In a one-shot-to-failure test (transverse axis shear), both designs are pretty close. In fatigue, the weld will crystallize before the assembled frame will fail. But I wouldn't worry about it. Either will do the job unless you carry 90 pounds regularly and drop your loaded packframe on one corner from the roof of your '62 Dodge panel truck before each trip just to warm it up. Of more significance than the welded versus assembled tempest in a Sierra cup is whether the particular frame that fits you is a good example of its type. Let's look at the welded frame first.

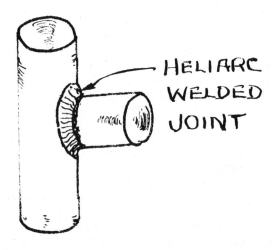

HELIARC WELDED JOINT

Find out whether it's really welded. A lot of frames *look* welded, but they're not — they're furnace-brazed. A good braze may be preferable to a crummy weld, but a brazed joint isn't as strong as a good weld. A braze depends on capillary flow of the braze metal into the interstices of the parent metal for its strength, and this is limited. You don't really melt the parent metal; you melt the braze metal enough to flow. Like supersolder, if you'll pardon the oversimplification. A weld, on the other hand, does melt the parent metal, so the fusion is complete. How can you tell the difference? Well, you could ask your outfitter. He should know. If you're still in doubt, look at the joint. A production furnace braze is usually done with a little fitted collar of braze metal that's melted by the furnace. The resulting job may be a bit bulgy, but it's generally smooth. A weld, on the other hand, usually has little marks on it.

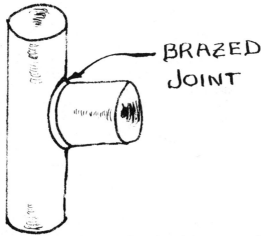

BRAZED
JOINT

If you looked at them closely, you'd find that they were tiny figures of eight, because that's the pattern a welder uses to do a tight, multipass weld on pipe. They may be ground a bit for cosmetic purposes, but they're never ground in a perfectly smooth fillet. It'd cost an arm and a leg!

A good weld on thin tubing should be performed under an inert gas blanket — helium being the commonest. This excludes oxygen from the weld, and in the process, eliminates skunky little inclusions of oxide particles that will corrode the joint in time. So if the manufacturer's blurb mentions "heliarc welded," this is righteous gear.

If you're packing heavy, or if you simply want your frame to last, the nearer to a box section the better. Avoid welded frames with only three crossmembers in general, and look for five in the larger sizes, with one very near to the top. Obviously, there can't be one at the bottom of the frame, because your butt has to fit somewhere in there. Yet a frame with a foot of unsupported tubing poking up into the air above the crossmember that the shoulder harness is hung from is weaker than the one that is tied together at the top. The unsupported tubes can bend more easily, resulting in more flex at the weld joints. Remember that a welded frame has to be more or less rigid to survive. If it's too wimpy, the welds fail a lot sooner due to crystallization.

The assembled frame ranges from junk that you'll find in discount houses to some superbly engineered gear using some exotic materials. I've carried the Alpine Designs frame, which is joined by Lexan fittings, for many miles without any trouble. A lot of dudes stick their noses up at any plastics, but this stuff (a polycarbonate developed by General Electric) is fully as strong as a weld, and is better in two areas — low temperature strength and fatigue properties. This isn't to say that Lexan can't be faulted. It can. Any molded plastic can be badly molded. However, a failed Lexan fitting, or a failed metal fitting on a Jan Sport, can be replaced. A failed weld is bye bye baby!

The major advantage to the assembled frame isn't strength. The better assembled frames are adjustable. In other words, the crossmember that mounts the shoulder straps can be slid up and down the side rails so that the frame can be tuned to your trembling torso with great precision.

SEWING STRAPS
INTO SHOULDER PADS

GOOD

GOOD

NOT
BAD

SCHLOCK!

There is one kind of assembled frame to avoid, as I said before. Usually it lives in discount houses. The crossmembers are chopped off, and plugged with some undefined plastic with a threaded hole in it. The crossmember is then fastened to the side rail by a bolt passing through a hole drilled in the side rail. They fall apart under a cross look!

So much for the basic frame. Now let's look at its rigging. First the shoulder pads. Are they well and truly attached to the crossmember? Clevis pins and split rings are fine. So are Jan Sport's doubly damned bolts. Are the grommets there to stay? Are they staked grommets that really grab the material? They should be. How about the pads themselves? Wide and thick and firm? Groovy. And the fabric covering? You want a good, sturdy packcloth. How about the straps themselves. Do they look like they'll wear well? Are the upper parts sewn well into the shoulder pad covers, or are they hung together with a stitch and a prayer? Is the bottom part attached to the packframe like it grew there or does it look flimsy?

Incidentally, several excellent frames, notably the Alp, fail miserably on this last point. A few minutes of work will rectify it. The textbook on how to make a super-durable shoulder strap arrangement was written by Kelty Pack. Even if the Big K doesn't fit you — and it doesn't fit me too well — a look at some of their construction details on their shoulder harness is rewarding. Big, meaty staked grommets; wide, firm closed cell foam pads; neat sturdy stitching where the upper strap is attached to the pad; a sturby Tabler buckle that adjusts easily and holds its position well, and a very secure U-ring fitting for the lower strap. A thoroughly workmanlike job that's virtually bombproof.

Okay, the shoulder strap arrangement seems substantial, easy to adjust, and comfortable? Fine. It should be possible to reposition the upper mounting in or out to accommodate different shoulder widths. If you can't do that, make sure that the pack fits well as it sits.

Backbands? There are a lot of different ideas about them, as you'll see when you look over the selection in any good shop. For years, the quality arrangement was a heavy, wide chunk of seat belt nylon tensioned either by cords or, with Camp Trails, an ingenious little turnbuckle gizmo. Either method works. Nylon does stretch, so you'll have to tighten the backbands occasionally to keep the crossmembers from playing a contradance on your spine. I've always liked the full-length mesh backband that Alp and Trailwise use on their frames, but some people feel that it compresses too much of your clothing against you and doesn't permit any ventilation. This is true, but you're not going to get much ventilation under any packframe. Go for comfort.

Some makers use a narrow band of nylon mesh; again, breathability is the reason. This arrangement is certainly the best for that purpose, but I'm not sure that breathability's that great a factor unless you're into winter conditions. The folks at Jan Sport believe in a most unbreathable padded backband. It's warm and damp, but by God it's comfortable. A lot of very experienced, very competent equipment designers have honest differences of opinion, and these extend to backbands on packframes. If it feels good on *you,* buy it – and to hell with your expert friend's advice. To hell with my advice, for that matter.

UPPER STRAP ATTACHMENT WITH CLEVIS. MOST PACKS ARE BUILT THIS WAY.

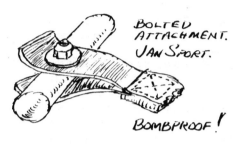

BOLTED ATTACHMENT. JAN SPORT.

BOMBPROOF !

METHODS FOR ATTACHING LOWER STRAPS TO FRAME

CLEVIS AND SPLIT RING. COMMONLY USED. IT WORKS.

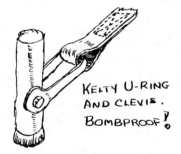

KELTY U-RING AND CLEVIS. BOMBPROOF !

The next item to check out is the waistbelt or hipbelt. To begin with, the padded belt offers a considerable boost in comfort. You need a frame with a padded belt, or one that will accommodate a padded belt later on when you have some extra cash. Not all padded belts are created equal, though. Some are poor, flimsy things with squlchy little blocks of open-cell foam that flatten out readily and absorb sweat and rainwater eagerly. A padded belt can be appraised like a shoulder harness. Is it wide enough to distribute the load evenly around your body? Great. Is the padding of closed-cell foam covered with a durable material? Fine. How about the buckle? Fastens easily and securely? Can you get out of the belt in a hurry? Does it adjust easily so you can alter the way you carry the pack a bit during a long day's journey? How long do you think the packframe will last? And finally, are you comfortable wearing it? You are? Neat-o. Looks like you found yourself a pack-frame.

Now, and only now, look at the bags you can get with the frame you can live with. If this sounds bass-ackwards to you, remind yourself that the bag is merely a container. The frame lives next to you, and it *must* be comfortable. The best packbag in the bloody universe is cold comfort if it's mounted on a frame that doesn't fit you. You must consider durability and usability in a pack bag. Separating out good fabric from schlock can be difficult, but you can assume that the better-known makers of packbags are using acceptable stuff. The "in" material now is Cordura, a beefy, rough-textured nylon duck that weighs in at about 10 ounces per yard. It's tough . . . and expensive. In general, I view it as over-kill, except for rucksacks that get thrown about a lot and snatched at by rocks and branches. The other common material is a 7.9 ounce nylon called Parapac. Both fabrics are coated with some sort of polymer to provide waterproofing.

A word on this waterproof jazz before we go any farther. No pack is completely waterproof. Zippers leak; seams leak; the spot where your stove has rubbed the bag for 200 miles leaks; the spot where the coating machinery blew it leaks. Let's say "water repellent" — maybe even "very water repellent". One major manufacturer, Kelty, still makes most of their bags in a 7-ounce fabric that is *not* coated, and their reasoning is as follows. A coated fabric, because it loads one thread at a time in a tear, is less strong than an uncoated fabric, where the shear load can be better distributed. They also feel that the uncoated bag permits some circulation of air so your funky damp socks won't grow green fur overnight.

I suppose that this is supportable scientifically, and some experience in the Sierras indicates that this is true for that delightfully dry climate, but for the Northeasterner? No sir! I've been on trips where my pipe tobacco got too soggy to light! An airy, breezy, well-ventilated packbag just doesn't mean too much to me. I should add, however, that Kelty pack fabric is very water-repellent, and nothing short of a downpour will soak through it. I use a "waterproof" pack-bag — with a raincover over it. Two layers of fabric are about 100 times better able to turn water than one, and the raincover doesn't get abraded by the spiky stuff you're carrying.

So much for waterproof bags and fabrics. If you're convinced that the fabric is acceptable, go on from there and look at the construction details. Are the pockets sewn on well, or do they look like a chipmunk could tear them off in a fit of blind rage? Are the pocket zippers sewn in well with sturdy thread, or will they peel easily. It's almost impossible to find a bad zipper today. This is a competitive market! No manufacturer of *anything* will buy a really bad zipper because he knows his stuff will come bounding back at him. Bad individual zippers are possible, but not poor design and construction in general. Check each zipper to see that it works well and smoothly.

Check out the way the seams are sewn on the bag. Bunchy, irregular, wandering stitches? You don't need that. It's more than ugly; it loads each stitch irregularly, and sooner or later (usually sooner) you'll pop one or more. Packs are sewn with heavy thread, so you don't need eight rows of stitching; but make sure what's there is well done.

If the pack has a hold-open frame, how is that attached? Sometimes it's merely dropped into little pockets sewn on the inside of the packbag. Now, a hold-open frame does more than hold the mouth of the bag open or make the bag look tidy. It soaks up a fair amount of loading. Plop ten pounds in the bottom of a packbag with a hold-open frame. You can feel the tension in the front panel of the bag which is pulling down on the hold-open frame. Fasten the hold-open frame bar *to the frame,* and reinforce the back panel where the bar gets tensioned with several rows of stitching and nylon tape in the seam. Otherwise, the bag will simply self-destruct.

Take a look at how the bag is attached to the frame. If it's grommeted and pinned with clevis pins, are the grommets brass, and are they attached securely to multiple layers of fabric? They should be. Is the uppermost grommet a staked grommet? It should be, because that's the one that receives the greatest loading. If the bag is attached by other means — and there are many, and more new ones monthly — does it look like the attachment method will stand the gaff of heavy use? If in doubt, ask your outfitter.

All right, the fabric's good, the zippers are good, and the bag is attached solidly to the frame. So far you're in good shape. If the bag's a conventional top-opener, take a good look at the flap that covers it. Is it long enough to cover a tent that you want to stow across the top of the pack? Most tents — and sleeping bags, for that matter — are put in stuff bags that are a bit wider than a backbag. Sure, you can tote them under the pack, or on the top bar if your pack is so equipped. Simple empiricism's the best test. Stuff the bag, and then plop a tent across it and see if the flap will cover it and the tie-downs are long enough to still tie down.

Let's take a look at packbag design. A simple open sack with four pockets that meets the criteria we've established will do the job for you, but there are some design embellishments that may enhance the pack's virtues in your eyes. The first is a divided bag. The upper part of the pack (usually about the upper two thirds) is separated from the lower part by a sewn-in panel, and the bottom part has a zipper opening. I like this convenience, by the way, because I can separate out little grotch that would normally wind up rattling around the bottom of the pack with stray flakes of tobacco, pine needles, and assorted dust woolies.

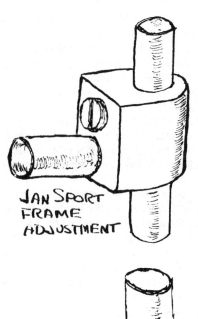

JAN SPORT
FRAME
ADJUSTMENT

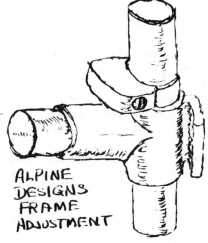

ALPINE
DESIGNS
FRAME
ADJUSTMENT

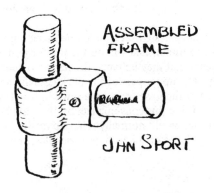

ASSEMBLED
FRAME

JAN SPORT

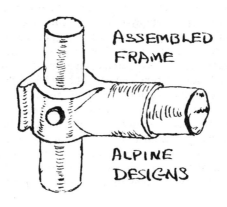

ASSEMBLED
FRAME

ALPINE
DESIGNS

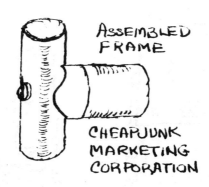

ASSEMBLED
FRAME

CHEAPJUNK
MARKETING
CORPORATION

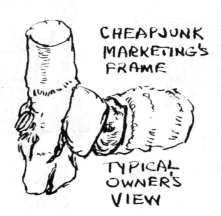

CHEAPJUNK
MARKETING'S
FRAME

TYPICAL
OWNER'S
VIEW

There are several distinct methods of engineering this bottom compartment, and we'll describe them by their manufacturer's names. Commonest is the Kelty-Camp Trails method, in which the bottom compartment is designed to carry small oddments, and the zipper simply runs across the back panel. The compartment's mouth isn't big enough for bulky items. The second is the Alpine Designs method, in which the zipper runs essentially all the way across the pack from frame rail to frame rail, and exposes a compartment big enough to put a small sleeping bag in. I like this type myself, but be advised that the zipper in this design takes all the loading, so don't fill up the compartment with rock samples. Make certain that the zipper is well stitched in place. The third is the Jan Sport method, which makes use of a halfmoon-shaped suitcase opening with a double zipper arranged in push-me pull-you fashion. I've used this zip style in my daybag and I like it. It gives either total access or accurate, ferret-it-out access. The latter is most handy in a downpour. It also provides a back-up zipper bug in case one fails, which may be a comfort to some troubled souls.

KELTY B-4
OPEN BAG & FRAME

KELTY TIOGA
DIVIDED BAG & FRAME

By the way, Jan Sport's design honcho, Murray Pletz, must be a remarkably perceptive dude. Having discovered at an early age that the item you want, even in a divided bag, is always at the bottom, some of his packbags are set up with a suitcase-opening back panel on the big upper compartment, with push-me, pull-you zippers, like my little daybag. How it would be in a downpour is questionable, but it surely does away with desultory rummaging. This feature is possibly less handy for the short trip than it is on a long slog where you're truly living out of your pack, but I found it so pleasant to use that I recently went out and bought the big D3 wraparound.

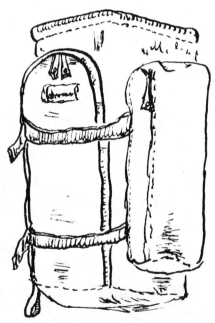

JAN SPORT
CASCADE PACKBAG

Now I'm not an expedition mountaineer, so I don't really need the massive leather crampon pad, nor do I really need the *two* ice axe straps — one for the long snowfield axe and one for the short technical axe. And I've always felt that wraparound frames were nice but not essential. Howbeit, this big mother is *comfortable,* and carries all the truck I need for family packing, and . . . Hell, I can't justify the purchase. It just felt right, that's all. I'd like it even better if I could get it away from my wife, who was massively indifferent until she tried it.

The moral of this little digression is threefold. One: if it's comfortable and usable, it's your bag — assuming it's well-made. Two: don't get so enamored of a particular feature that it blinds you. Three: if what you have does the job for you, why buy a duplicate? I have an Alp Expedition that I've beat hell out of for four years, Lexan couplings and all.

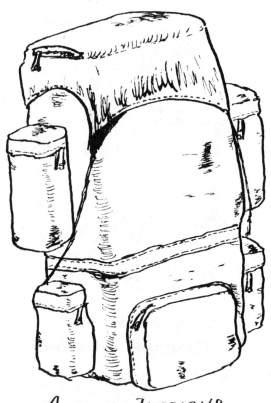

ALPINE DESIGNS
EXPEDITION PACKBAG

GERRY VAGABOND

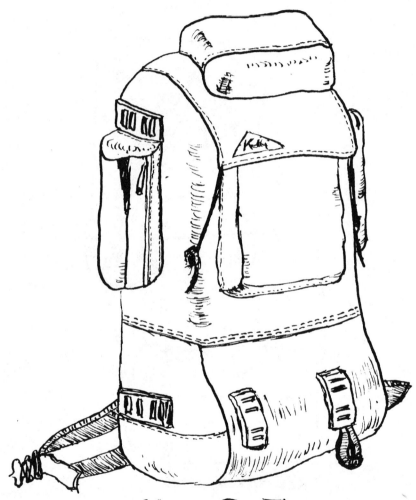

KELTY SKI TOUR

THE SOFT PACK REVOLUTION

There was a time when everybody backpacked with rucksacks, great shapeless bags that punished your shoulders and ate your spine before midmorning snack time. A few daring souls used the Trapper Nelson packframe, but the rucksack was the only way to suffer for most of Europe and North America. Then along came the tubular aluminum packframe, and rucksacks vanished almost overnight. A few traditionalists used them, of course, and a few people who practiced the arcane sport of cross-country skiing returned to the rucksack after learning that skiing with a frame pack on is like skiing in a body cast.

Climbers used them because they clung well to the body and followed your moves closely. The relentlessly creative Gerry Cunningham, who cheerfully violated many of the "traditions" he helped to create in backpacking, tried his hand at a contemporary rucksack, a horizontally-compartmented unit similar to his CWD frame pack bag. A lot of people looked at the bag, called the Vagabond, and liked the idea. It carried well with about twenty pounds on board, clung to your back, followed your movements well, and nothing hung out on top or at the sides. They liked the elegant engineering solution to weight control as well. They stood in line in admiration, but they didn't buy many of them.

Still, it started a lot of people thinking. Then came the boom in cross-country skiing. Along with it came a vast migration of young people across the country by thumb. A frame pack's a horror when you're on skis, and when the back seat of a Volksie is filled up if you're hitch-hiking. Wow! Now you could build a second-generation rucksack with some hope of selling the thing.

And they did, beginning with Justus Bauschinger's imaginative Ruthsac for North Face. After that, the deluge. The North Face Kak Sack; an array of Bauschinger-designed gear from Class Five, with delightful names like Quimex, Backex and Better Mousetrap; the big Kelty Ski Tour; a host of subframe and external frame ruckers from Jan Sport; superspecialist packs like the Chouinard Ultima Thule and Don Jensen's Rivendell, both climbing packs, and an incredibly rugged subframe pack from Alpenlite designed as a "ready pack" for some California search and rescue teams; and that's only a few.

They don't feel like the rucksacks of yore, believe me. They're not as comfortable as a frame pack with a heavy load, and because they hang closer, they hang sweatier. But their aluminum bow backstays transfer some weight to those big padded waistbelts, and the bags are very tough. You can go through brush wearing one; you can ski with one.

They're not a beginner's pack, though. I still view them as essentially the province of the specialist – and the European walking tourist. But if you have needs that a frame pack won't fill, look at these big dudes. Look closely. Evaluate them like you'd evaluate a frame pack for workmanship and comfort. And when you find one you really like, then we'll do a *real* bushwhack.

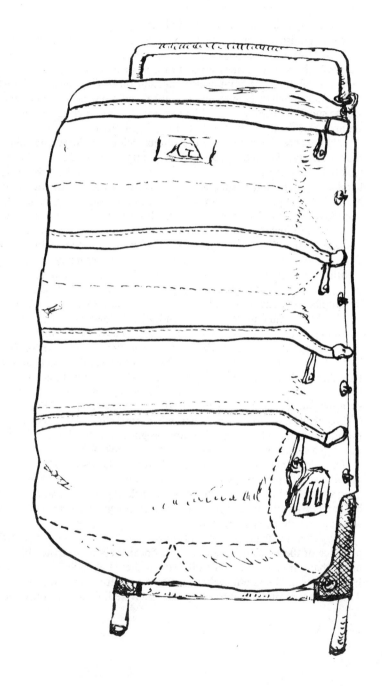

AN UNUSUAL DESIGN. THREE HORIZONTAL
COMPARTMENTS FOR CONTROLLED WEIGHT PACKING.
AND A BIG BOTTOM COMPARTMENT FOR YOUR BAG.

5. PACKIN' YOUR GEAR

> *"There were five million hogs and six*
> *million dogs*
> *and seven million barrels of porter,*
> *There were eight million sides of old*
> *blind horses' hides*
> *In the hold of the Irish Rover."*
> Old Irish Folk Song

There's a travel game that my old man played with me when we'd take a long auto trip, back in the dim and distant 30's. It was called, "I packed my grandmother's trunk," and it went something like this. One person would start it off with a line like, "I packed my grandmother's trunk with a jar of Keiller's Dundee Marmalade," and the next person would pick it up with, "I packed my grandmother's trunk with a jar of Keiller's Dundee Marmalade and the collected poems of Lydia Sigourney." The next person would add another item, something commonplace like, "une voiturette marque Lancia," and so on, until grandmother's trunk was packed with the most bizarre oddments in the bloody universe. It's a great game, and I play it with my tribe today (would you believe "a red Italian racing grinch bicycle"?), but we don't play it when we're packing our packs for a weekend in the boondocks!

You wouldn't believe the quantities of useless grotch I see people toting into the wilds each weekend. Cans of soda, transistor radios, huge battery-powered lanterns, six changes of clothing, and a beach umbrella are obvious surplusage, and I know that you're not going to take that sort of stuff. But you'd be amazed at how much stuff gets toted into the outback that simply isn't necessary. Simple things. Coffee, for instance. If I take the time to measure out a heavy coffee ration (say six cups of Maxim freeze-dried a day) into a Ziploc bag, I wind up with a superlight little packet. If I just toss a 2/3 filled jar of Maxim in the pack, not only am I taking ten times the amount of coffee I need, but I'm also carrying a big, fat, breakable jar. That's one example: Now consider sugar, tea, powdered milk, cocoa, crunchy-munchy type cereal, and other such things that like to get loose and run around your pack. Do you begin to see the advantages of repackaging? Succinctly stated, it's pounds, not ounces. That's worth the hassle.

In a similar vein, a small stove like a Svea 123 will burn a tankful (a third of a pint) in about 50 minutes at full throttle. Even if you're into six course meals, 50 minutes of cooking should get you through a supper. If you do a cold lunch, a full stove and a pint bottle of fuel should get you through a weekend. I can spill things by thinking about it; so I use a pint and a half container. It also gives me a surplus to give to some dude who's run out. But I don't need a quart of fuel, not by a long shot. The saving is well over half a pound in weight and enough space for a change of socks.

Let's not kid ourselves about all the "reduce the weight" guff you're confronted with in every backpacking book (including this one) and every catalog. Sure, it's important to keep the weight of each item in control if you can without fracturing your finances or without having blown so much cash for a super sleeping bag that you're forced to backpack in zoris. But it is far more important to adopt the philosophy of some eminent woodchucks like Thoreau and Han-shan and come to grips with what you don't need.

I've backpacked with a lot of superlight freaks, guys who cut the labels out of their jockey shorts and drill holes in their toothbrush handles, and I've seen them sweating with 45 pounds of superlight conveniences while I bump along with 25 pounds including my goddamn cameras. It's insidious! "Well, my portable, magnesium-lithium-aluminum alloy, battery-powered expedition-grade corncob weighs only 3.274 ounces, so I'll take it." And the next thing you know, you've added 20 pounds of superlight garbage that didn't have to be there in the first place.

Take what your body needs and your soul requires, and be a bit ruthless with your soul. Mine survives with a small notebook and a pencil stub, although on a long trip I indulge it with a skinny book of poems, usually Gary Snyder's. But that's indulgence. I have my own head to come to grips with or to ignore as I choose, and there are times when I'd sooner groove on my muscles and the thump of my heart and the cool air tearing at my throat and the million little impressions that a busy week has kept my body from receiving. My head will keep.

What you need is food, clothing, and shelter. While I carry some extra food in case I mess up my knee and have to lay over somewhere an extra day, it's not much food. I can live on what my body's stored for a long time; so extra food, except in winter, isn't a requirement. You don't need a sweater, a wool shirt, and a down jacket all at once. Hell, if it's cold enough to need both, get in your sleeping bag! You don't need a poncho, a rain jacket and a windbreaker. Take a rain jacket and let it do double duty. You don't need five pots and a full set of tableware, nor do you need a fresh change of clothes every day.

An ambulance-sized first aid kit isn't necessary for an easy weekend on well worn trails, although if I'm off on a one week solo bushwhack I may take a more extensive layout. I don't need an axe or a saw, and I don't need both a belt knife and pocket knife. One will do. I prefer the latter. You won't be stabbing anything more dangerous than peanut butter. I do carry a sharpening stone; a little one which I use as a pleasant, moronic time-killer while the pot's boiling. Boot dressing isn't necessary, for my boots are treated before I set out on the trail.

I've been carrying on for some time now about how not to pack your grandmother's trunk, and I've been nothing but uppity about it. My old lady and I just came back from an overnight trip, and our packs are sitting in the kitchen. Let's start with hers. In case you're curious, I'll mention brand names where applicable.

Molly's using my old Alp Sport frame and a battered Alp Expedition bag that's an honest-to-goodness veteran. Strapped to the frame under the bag is a Camp 7 North Col down bag in its stuff sack (a Sierra West stuff bag, because it's very rugged) and rolled up tightly next to the bag is a 48-inch long, one and a half inch thick open celled foam pad, covered with waterproof nylon on the bottom and sides, and polyester/cotton on the top. I think it's an Alp, but the label's long since been torn off.

Inside the pack's header flap is a Sierra Designs cagoule, which could best be described as a waterproof maxi dress with a hood. Opening the pack, we find a polybag filled with other people's litter, the poles and stakes for our old Gerry Yearound, a dead pair of wool socks and a very dead pair of wool inner socks, and a blue Sierra Designs Sierra Jacket with a busted zipper. The zipper's been busted for three years – a collie pup got to it – but the jacket closes nicely with snaps, so she's never gotten around to replacing the zipper. There's also a Sierra cup and a tablespoon and a small plastic bowl. In one side pocket is a pint and a half fuel bottle for our stove, and the other side pocket holds a one-liter poly water bottle. The lower (and smaller) side pockets hold a small flashlight (Mallory, AA cell, all 3 ounces of it), a small stuffbag containing some adhesive bandages, salt tablets, a tube of Chap-Stick, a needle and thread, a few aspirin, a bottle of sun screen (Class Five, a very protective lotion because she's fair skinned), insect repellent, some waterproof matches, and Moleskin.

This is obviously where any necessary medicines belong. I've been out on too many search operations caused by some dude forgetting his insulin or thyroid or nitroglycerin. Also, if I had a ten dollar bill for every kid conceived under the fragrant pines because some folks forgot their favorite contraceptive method, I wouldn't have to write books for a living. When you pass around the proverbial loaf of bread and jug of wine, you can relax and be mindless. Just keep your head buttoned when it's time to pass the thou.

The rear pocket holds a small zippered plastic envelope containing a notebook, pencil, maps, compass, matches and a whistle. This envelope and the stuffbag of miscellaneous medicines and repair items also go with her on daytrips. They're all together, easy to grab, and difficult to forget. The bottom compartment of her big packbag contains a very light wool long john top (Norwegian-made, very soft), a tennis hat, underpants, and a polybag with sanitary napkins in it.

She began the trip wearing G.I. fatigues and a fishnet shirt. On a longer trip, she'd take a lightweight polyester/cotton shirt as well for sun and bug protection. She carries a small pocket knife on a lanyard, and some toilet paper in a Ziploc bag in one of the big cargo pockets. The other cargo pocket is used for trail munchies for both of us. She has hypoglycemia, so she requires a steady supply of small amounts of protein-rich food. Her choice is peanuts augmented with cheese and beef jerky. The peanuts and the jerky live in that pocket, so they're accessible for munching.

The food she carried in her pack is gone now, of course, but if you're curious, she carried Sunday's breakfast (Granola and freeze-dried Mexican omelette), the coffee, sugar and powdered milk, and the inevitable packet of Wyler's lemonade mix. I carried Saturday's dinner (franks and beans, freeze dried, and butterscotch pudding), lunch fixin's (cheddar cheese, beef stick, pepperoni and Triscuits), and a half-liter of red wind in a polybottle, because this was a short trip.

My pack, an Alpine Designs expedition bag and adjustable frame, had a relatively bulky polyester mummy sleeper lashed onto the top bar. It's a Trail Tech Omni-Temp, warm to about 15 degrees, and at 4 lb. 14 oz., it's well over a pound heavier than my wife's North Col or my Sierra Designs 100 Superlight, but I thought it would be very wet (it wasn't), and chose the little Polarguard mummy. An Ensolite pad (3/8 inch thick, 63 inches long) is lashed to the frame beneath the packbag. It should be removed now and brushed off, because I used it as a trailside lounging mat on the way out, and the ground was pretty soggy. I'll probably forget, but I should do it now. I did unpack the sleeping bag and air it out as soon as we got in the house, but somehow I forgot the pad.

In one of the upper side pockets is my Svea 123 in its stuff bag. The spare parts for the stove are in the stuff bag too. So are matches. The other pocket holds a one-liter water bottle like Molly's. The upper compartment of the big pack holds our old Gerry Yearound tent and fly (Molly took the poles). The tent's placed crossways, at the very top of the bag. Beneath it, from left to right, is a stuffsack containing my old Sierra Jacket, a larger sack that holds two small nesting pots, a small tube of Trak soapless soap, a pot scrubber, a pot lifter, some aluminum foil, and a Bull Durham sack with spice vials in it, and finally another stuffsack that once held our food but now holds foil wrappers and such, besides a dead pair of wool socks and liner socks. Yeah, I'd better get them out of there. Otherwise, they'll march out and announce themselves in two days.

In the header pocket on the cover flap is a zippered plastic bag stuffed with a notebook, pencil, maps, thermometer, compass and matches. We'd share maps and compass on a long trip, but it's easier to just snatch your own envelope of gear than go through some involved checklist routine. This little envelope contains some of my favorite outdoor toys — the thermometer and an exercise in overkill called the Silva 15 TD-CL compass. Molly wouldn't be caught dead with the thermometer, and she knows that her Silva Polaris compass is as useful as my fatso for normal navigation. It just isn't as much fun, that's all. Big Blue, my Gerry All-Weather rain parka, also lives in the header, along with a pair of Sierra West rainchaps.

The big bag's lower compartment contains a Stil-Long shirt like Molly's, a small candle lantern, and two candles. It also held our lunch goodies, because they're easy to get at there, and it held my extra socks on the way in. The lower side pockets hold my own emergency gear in a stuff bag (aspirin, adhesive bandages, Moleskin, a few Darvon caps, a Chap Stick, and Lomotil tabs), twenty-five feet or so of parachute cord, and a little Mallory flashlight with spare AA cells and a spare bulb. We didn't need both lights, but they were both packed. Had we walked in on Friday night, one light would have stayed home and I would have taken the carbide lamp, which I prefer, or the Justrite electric headlamp, which Molly prefers. By the way, the switches of both flashlights were taped in "off" position.

There's not much in the back pocket of the big pack today. Insect repellent, a few pipe cleaners, some Brindley's Mixture and a corncob to put it in, and matches. A few things live in my pants pockets: a Swiss knife on a lanyard, toilet paper in a Ziploc bag, peanuts for munching, and a big red bandanna that serves as dishrag, sweatband, tourniquet, washcloth and towel. And that's it. There's not very much at all.

You may have noticed a certain progression in the way my pack was arranged. The Polarguard mummy sleeper was on top, and so was the tent. The food, the water, the stove, the fuel — all weighty for their volume — were also packed high in the bag and close to my body. Remember, you're happiest with a load on top of your head, and the backpacker's rule of "heavy hangs high and close" is the nearest approximation you can make.

If we had taken a longer trip, we would have added a few more items beyond extra food and fuel, but very little. Another change of socks, a paperback book apiece, a pair of moccasins, and maybe a camera or two. Sometimes I'll take a trail guide along, even though I know the country well, just to browse in. Maybe I'll take a fly rod and reel and a few flies. All of this, unless we take our whole array of cameras, doesn't amount to five pounds split between us. In short, we've packed our trunks with enough to keep us warm, dry, well-fed, and comfortable. We haven't duplicated our comfort items, and we've gone on the assumption that the countryside (and the company) is the entertainment.

This hasn't happened overnight. I've arrived at how to pack my grandmother's trunk by a long process of trial and error that began with my first trip into Lake Colden, in the heart of the High Peaks region of the Adirondacks. Colden's overrun with bodies now, but it wasn't then, and the old trail was narrow and dry, not a wide hogwallow churned endlessly by the relentless track of man. I was twelve, a pitiful stick figure of a kid, and I had what must have been all my worldly goods in an Adirondack pack basket. Clint West, for over twenty years the keeper of the gates at Colden, took one look at me as I dragged across the clearing to his cabin, and allowed as how I was carrying a fool's load. He advised me to empty out that groaning pack basket when I got back, putting everything I didn't use in one pile, and everything used in another. He went on to tell me to discard all of the first pile and half of the second. The first pile went easily, but it's taken me twenty-eight years to make inroads in the second one. Clint's a long time dead, but his quiet competence and gentle advice educated a whole generation of hard-core Adirondack bushwhackers. May it educate you in turn.

That's how I learned. Other people may be of a more orderly turn of mind, and have a learning curve that's not as unutterably flat as mine. One of my hiking companions, a totally competent engineering manager, maintains a list of his summer gear and his winter gear, and further divides that into day tripping gear and overnighting gear. Each list has been typed and Xeroxed. He checks off each item used on each trip, and makes notes on its performance, state of repair, and such. The lists are filed in a notebook and reviewed before each trip. It's a marvellously complete record of the process by which one man has refined and defined his needs.

Let me tell you, friend, it's a great comfort to do a trip with George. He always has what's needed. I can be counted on to bring a grapefruit as a surprise for breakfast — and forget the coffee. The last time I packed my grandmother's trunk, I left behind the collected poems of Lydia Sigourney, the Sweet Singer of Hartford.

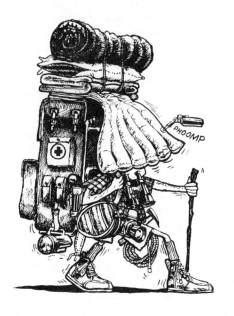

6. ALL ABOUT BAGS

"That's the kind of bag I'm in."
— Fred Neal

What you're simply trying to do is to come up with something readily transportable and lightweight that will keep you warm and dry and comfortable at night. The problem's complicated a bit by widely varying temperatures, by the fact that you're tired and producing less heat than usual, and by the fact that the sleeping body requires more insulation to maintain a normal temperature than an active body does. What really complicates the problem, moreover, is metabolism.

To begin with, let's see what temperatures we face in the East for what we euphemistically call three-season backpacking. Nights may range in the upper 70's, or they may dip to 10 above zero, but 15 to 20 would be more realistic. The Army Quartermaster Corps tells us that one inch of insulation – *any* insulation – will buy the average sleeping person 40 degrees of protection. That means that you'll maintain a normal 98.6 degree body temperature at 58.6 degrees, give or take a little. Now the QMC is an impressive data bank for such stuff. They're pretty experienced outfitters, after all. But their concept of what's sufficiently comfortable to enable some poor soul to be an effective troop and my concept of a comfortable night's sleep are rather at variance.

A more reasonable figure, and a fairly standard one in the industry, is about 27 degrees of protection per inch of insulation in a sleeping bag, and add another 5 degrees of protection if the bag has a hood. In other words, a mummy bag with 6 inches of overall thickness (that's 3 inches on top – what's underneath in the bag doesn't matter much) protects you 27 times 3 degrees, or 81 degrees. The bag would be warm to 17.6 degrees then. Knock off another 5 for a hood, and we're down to 12.6 degrees. Call it 15 to be on the conservative side, and about 90 percent of humanity will sleep comfortably in that bag at that temperature. A tent or a good windbreak will buy you about 10 degrees more, and as you're most likely going to be using a tent, a bag that's rated at 20 to 25 degrees should be more than adequate.

It's not quite that simple, but accept this for now. It's a good working generalization that I'll refine later, when you have more information to work with. In the meanwhile, you're going to be looking for a sleeping bag that will keep you cozy at 20 to 25 degrees, or a bit less if the weight of your purse permits. Tell somebody that and listen to the comments. In fact, you've maybe heard them already, but listen again.

"Don't get a mummy bag. They're uncomfortable."
"Goose down's the best by far."
"Don't buy anything that doesn't have white goose down in it."
"You want AAA grade down."
"Ripstop nylon's the only good covering material."
"Stay away from synthetics. They're no good."
"You'll need a bag with two and a half pounds of down in it."
"Watch out for nylon zippers. They're no good."
"You'll be too hot on a warm night."
"You can't wash a sleeping bag, and dry cleaning's expensive."

Not one of the above statements is true; yet a lot of people who should know better will pronounce them with that stateliness reserved for holy writ. Let's really look at sleeping bags, so you have some basis for decision when you're faced with an array of them at your outfitter's.

INSULATION AND FILLING

I've indicated that a bag in the 20°-25° range is adequate for most three-season backpacking, and a bag that will keep you warm at that temperature should be 5 inches thick overall, when it's fluffed up a bit. If you want to be on the safe side, or have additional bucks to burn, shoot for 10-15 degrees and about 6 inches of thickness. Thickness, or *loft* in the jargon of the trade, is the key. Essentially, you're buying your insulation from a layer of uncirculating ("dead") air, and the insulation value is a function of thickness alone. You obviously want an insulation material that is light, compressible, and able to return to its original volume time after time after being compressed for carrying. The optimum material for this is goose down, but whether goose down suits *your* needs is worth a closer look.

There's no mystery about down, although you wouldn't know that by reading catalogs. It comes from waterfowl — geese and ducks — waterfowl raised for slaughter, which probably accounts for about ten percent of the market value of the beast. When a manufacturer states that his bags are filled with "prime Northern goose down," he's not telling you anything that has any standing in law except that most of the down is goose down, and that there is no more than 20 percent of small feathers. "Prime," if it's an honest statement, means down from mature birds, and "Northern" means that the down comes from birds raised in a four-season climate where their down plumules are plumper and more resilient. Frankly, it doesn't matter at all. Bag manufacturers buy their down from down processors. They buy a grade of down that is specified by filling power, resiliency, percentage of feathers, and oil content. The processor creates a blend of downs to arrive at the specification.

Let's look at these terms a bit more closely, because they're really the keys to knowing something about down. "Filling power" is a measurement of how much volume a given unit weight of down will expand to fill. In its crudest form, it's a measurement of "loft", but it doesn't tell you anything about durability. An ounce of a very good blend of goose down will expand to about 535 cubic inches, while a high-grade duck down will expand to about 10 percent less, or in the neighborhood of 470-475 cubic inches. Obviously, there is some down available that will loft to fantastic volume, well over 600 cubic inches per ounce. It is cruelly expensive, and is used as a blending down only in the best grades of down. In the past, a filling power of 550-575 was not unheard of, but one of those odd causality chains that crops up now and then has made really high-loft down a thing of the past.

Down-filled sleeping bags and garments have increased in popularity in the past five years at an incredible rate. In the meantime, Northern Europe, where the best down has come from, has seen the aftermath of deep political and social changes that resulted, among other things, in a reduction in the size of the average family. In the past, the average market-sized goose was a two or three year bird of 25 pounds or more. This size was optimum for a large family – and it produced dense down pods with heavy plumules. The standard market bird of today is nearer 12 pounds. The down pods are less full; the plumules are thinner. The down lofts less.

The manufacturer can't live with just a loft rating on his down, because you can run mediocre down through a perchlorethylene bath (ordinary dry-cleaning solvent, called "perk" in the trade), strip it of all its natural oils, and it will loft to hell and gone. It will also crumble quickly and lose its insulating value, and it will lose its ability to spring back to shape after it's compressed. So the manufacturer tests for resiliency by a standard test method developed by the Army QMC, and tests for oil content. The latter is ticklish. There's no absolutely reliable test for oil content, although there are several that offer reasonable indications. An experienced person can judge oil content as satisfactory or not by feel. It's that same sort of mystical process like coffee blending, in a way. Too much oil will result in down that mats and clumps too easily, rebounds slowly, and smells like something died inside a baffle tube. Too little oil simply means that the down will disintegrate. One to one and a half percent by weight is about optimum. This is enough to keep the down from disintegrating, enough to lubricate the fibers so that they'll rebound well without internal friction, and not so much as to inhibit loft by matting.

As I said before, down is a blended product, and there are many steps in its processing. "Raw" down arrives in bales, and to say that they're pretty rank would be an exercise in gross understatement. The down is steam-cleaned and sterilized, which removes a lot of the crud. After drying, it's blown into a column that functions like a fractionating tower at an oil refinery. The fine plumules settle out very slowly, the less plump ones settle out more quickly, and the feathers more quickly still. Trash, of course, falls to the bottom with a dull thud. If you exhaust a portion of the column, you'll suck out down of a certain gross grade. Repeat that process a few times, and you wind up with several distinct grades. Small-lot blending will determine how much of each is needed to arrive at a certain filling power for those lots of down. Even the finest grades of down will contain some small feathers, and it's desirable that they do. The small feathers act like little paddles to keep the down from bunching and matting. Cheaper grades may contain more feathers and/or larger feathers, and the cheapest grades of "goose down" may contain 72 percent goose down, the rest being duck down and feathers.

It should be evident from the above that a high-grade duck down may well be preferable to a run-of-the-mill goose down. Unless you find a legitimate sale, a bag containing really good down, duck or goose, will cost substantially more than a bag containing ordinary or sub-par down, assuming a reasonable parity in construction techniques.

Consider a synthetic insulation. In the past, if you said "synthetic" to a backpacker, he'd choke on his pipe from laughing. You know the bags he was thinking of. They still exist. They're covered in some coarse material, and lined in flannel with pheasant flapping around on them. They have cute little roofs that can be erected, by some magical process, over the head of the intrepid outdoorsman. They're two inches thick and eight pounds heavy, and they're great if you need to lie down on cold ground to do a value adjustment on your Volksie. As backpacking bags they're monstrosities.

All that nonsense has changed dramatically, due to the increasing cost of down and the increasing technical involvement in backpacking of two giant outfits, Du Pont and Celanese. Du Pont's walked in the door with something called Fiberfill II, and Celanese has turned up with a mouthful called Celanese Fortrel Polarguard. ™   They're both polyester materials, and quite similar in the properties that might concern you. There the similarity ends. Polarguard is a continuous-filament fiber, while Fiberfill II is a chopped fiber. A quick look at the manufacturing methods might be illuminating. Both are produced like a spider sends out a web; in fact, the device that makes the filaments is called a spinneret. The spider makes one filament at a time; Du Pont and Celanese do a bit better. As these polyester strands are extruded through the spinneret, Celanese spins them in a huge, loose rope called a "tow". This tow is then blown open by air pressure and the filaments are picked up on a set of rollers and rolled into an endless mat of continuous fibers. The primary orientation is lengthwise, of course, but the filaments are crimped to give them a built-in, permanent "bounce", and the lengthwise orientation isn't perfect, and isn't intended to be. Some crossing is desirable to keep the mat from separating and developing cold spots.

Fiberfill II, on the other hand, is chopped into short fibers (about 7 inches long) when it comes from the spinneret. Actually, "chopped" isn't the word. Polarguard is a solid filament, but Fiberfill II is a hollow filament. Its ends are somewhat pinched off to eliminate moisture absorption. The shoft fibers are then baled up and sent off to intermediate processors who run the bales through a machine that insures a random orientation of the fibers. This provides a way of keeping the insulation from separating and developing cold spots. Some huge manufacturers do their own *cardinetting,* as this process is called, but most rely on processors for their Fiberfill II.

These materials offer some outstanding advantages to the Northeasterner. Their moisture absorption is less than one half of one percent, which means that once you've squeezed out the water trapped in the interstices of the mat, and shaken the bag to remove excess water from the shell, you have a damp but viable sleeper that will dry easily in the air or from your body heat with no discernible loss of loft. Down, on the other hand, is impossible to dry in the field in any reasonable time. My own experience is that it takes three or four days to thoroughly air-dry a laundered down bag, although it could be used before that time in an emergency. There's no doubt about it. Polyester offers a considerable advantage of reliability in a wet environment. You can sleep comfortably in a sopping wet polyester bag a half-hour after immersion, and that's a great safety and convenience factor.

In terms of insulation value per unit weight, the polyesters still can't compare to down, but they're getting close. According to Du Pont's rather conservative figures, prime down (550 loft) has it over Fiberfill II by a margin of 1 to 1.4. In other words, a two-pound down bag would have to be replaced by a Fiberfill II bag of about 2 pounds 12 ounces. Another measurement of insulating value, the Army's Clo unit, shows the synthetics to be almost 90 percent as effective as down, and more effective than the old Army 50/50 down and feather mixture.

The new synthetics are very effective, lightweight insulation. They're heavier per unit warmth, as it were, but this is reduced a bit in a finished bag because you don't need the amount of fabric in a polyester bag. They're compressible, too. Not as compressible as down, but about 90% as compressible – if you're strong! This means that you need a stuff bag about an inch fatter. You can get a damn fine polyester mummy bag for forty-eight bucks at present prices, and comparable warmth from a downie will run close to a hundred. The difference is the price of a pack-frame; so look over this stuff.

While the synthetics offer considerable value, and that lovely "warm when wet" property, a good down bag is still the proven choice of backpackers. A good bag is still difficult to select because so much that's really important is hidden. Before we get down to the nitty-gritty of final selection, let's look at a few design concepts.

Bags (down or synthetic) are divided into three types: the mummy, the square-cut (or mostly square-cut), and the square-cut with a hood. Between ourselves, there isn't a choice. I see no virtue to a square-cut bag, and only a little more to a square-cut with a hood. The mummy's my choice, for a lot of reasons.

1. The mummy's tapered, contoured shape permits less circulation air around your sleeping body. Dead air is warm air, circulating air isn't.
2. The mummy's hood buys you a conservative five degrees over a comparable bag without a hood. I'd be inclined to say it buys more, because about fifteen percent of your heat transfer mechanism is your scalp and neck.
3. The mummy bag, being a bit slimmer, is a better configuration for controlling down shifting. More on this later.
4. The better mummy bags actually offer **more** foot room than the seemingly larger square-cuts.
5. The mummy's a lot warmer, pound for pound. There may be a half-pound difference (or more) between a 15-degree mummy and a 15-degree square-cut.
6. In deference to the square-cut design, it has a zipper that runs around the foot, so the bag can be opened flat and used as a quilt. In these days of ripoff fuel oil prices, this has been a decided asset in our house. Our old barrel-shaped bags have seen an honorable revival. But the mummy is designed to allow a left zip and a right zip bag to be zipped together if you're into the compatibility trip. It's still a more efficient unit than two square-cuts zipped together.

If you have any doubts about the mummy configuration, or if you've been frightened at an impressionable age by the old envelope-foot GI bags, your friendly local outfitter will be glad to let you crawl into a mummy (just take your shoes off first) and wiggle around. He may even rent sleeping bags, in which case you can try one for a weekend. I'm not saying that all you mummy-haters will be convinced, but most of you will. Betcha!

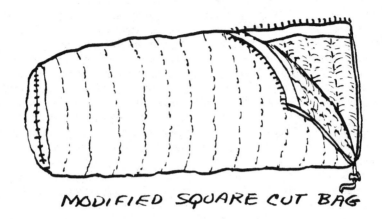

MODIFIED SQUARE CUT BAG

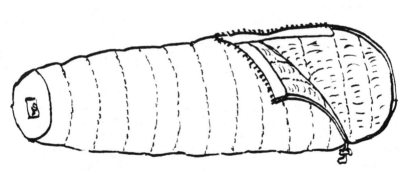

MUMMY BAG

So there you are, standing around in stocking feet at your outfitter's, looking at six different models of bags all of which are warm enough for you, and all of which seem to fit you. From the outside, they look pretty much alike. But the prices range from just over seventy bucks to just over a hundred and ten. Let's look at these bags, and try to account for the price differences so you'll know what you're buying.

Let's begin with the obvious — fabric. The most commonly used material for quality sleeping bag shells is ripstop nylon. It's a distinctive weave, developed for aerial tow targets, and you can recognize it by its distinctive square grid pattern. Ripstop is woven with several threads twisted together to form that heavy, relatively bombproof grid line. The areas in between are filled with a single-thread weave. As with tents, it's almost impossible to separate out the first-rate fabrics from the bad ones by casual inspection. Unless you actually count threads, there's precious little visible difference between a weave with 110 threads in the warp and 90 — except that the latter is a lot cheaper. Your best visual clues to fabric adequacy are empirical. The fabric must breathe; otherwise your sweat will condense on the inner layer of fabric and soak the insulation. As we've observed, down is very unhappy when wet and somewhat unhappy when damp. Grab a chunk of the bag, flatten it out over your mouth, and try to suck air through it. Then it's not so tight as to be effectively impermeable. Now look over the bag. If there are tiny pinfeathers and down pods poking out of it in lots of places, the fabric isn't downproof. This can happen in the best-regulated mills, because nylon is a stretchy material that's extremely sensitive to loom tension. As you're trying to produce a fabric that's tight enough to contain down, but not so tight as to preclude breathing, all you need is a little slip in tension and the fabric doesn't make it. A few small feathers inevitable (and desirable) in a down blend may poke through off and on. Grab the little beast from the opposite side and pull it back *into* the bag. That's all.

Another common fabric, especially in the lower-priced bags, is nylon taffeta. While ripstop is woven in a one over/one under pattern, taffeta is woven in a two or more over/one under pattern, which accounts for a smoother finish. Contrary to popular belief, a look at Army QMC data shows that taffeta is stronger than ripstop, breathes better, and is more abrasion-resistant. Why, then, has taffeta been superseded as a covering for high quality sleepers? Two reasons, really. The first is that taffeta will run more readily than ripstop, and a tear will propagate more easily. Ripstop offers better protection against catastrophic failure, in other words. Also when ripstop was first introduced, the serious backpacker and mountaineer greeted it with hosannahs. It became *the* fabric for quality sleeping bags, and blew everything else off the market. The mountaineer was attracted to its bombproof qualities, to be sure, but also to its light weight. Downproof taffeta usually weighs about 2.2 ounces per square yard, while the most common ripstop weight is a 1.9 ounce fabric, and 1.5 ounce is common on expedition-grade equipment. Seven tenths of an ounce per yard doesn't seem like much, but a winter bag may contain over 8 yards of fabric. That's six ounces less that you have to truck to the top of the continent. Also, the lighter fabric doesn't inhibit the loft of the down as much. All these factors contributed to the ripstop explosion, and while 1.9 ounce ripstop is probably the optimum sleeping bag fabric, 2.2 ounce taffeta would do the job for less money if you're not fussy about a little extra weight. The problem is that your better bags in terms of internal construction are all done in ripstop, with taffeta being relegated to the less sophisticated sacks.

Another obvious difference is the zipper. Again, while all zippers are good, there are some that have proven to be stronger and more reliable. These are *big* zippers, like the Talon ladder coil, the Opta Coil and the Big #10 YKK. They're more expensive than the smaller coils and the #5 and #7 YKK's are usually set up in a double-pull, separating configuration. This means that you can separate the zipper at the foot, and zip your bag to another bag. It also means that when your feet get too warm, you can unzip the sack from the bottom up. This ventilation game works whether you're in the sack alone, or two bags are zipped together. It's a desirable feature, and a lot of the less expensive bags don't have it. You pay for it, though.

While you're looking at that zipper, notice what's connected to it to see the difference between a primo bag and a run of the mill bag. A zipper is that which leaks air in the night, and the bag designer has provided a sort of seal in the form of a down-filled tube called a draft tube or draft flap. It usually hangs down over the zipper, but it need not, contrary to belief, if it's big enough. Look at the flap on a top-line bag. It's *big*, it's thick, and covers the zipper with a lot to spare. The zipper's also sewn onto the outer shell with two rows of stitching. The cheaper bag's draft flap is a separate tube, and it and the zipper are sewn to the edge of the bag. You might also notice a difference in the flap itself. Cheapies have skimpy little things that barely cover the zipper, and the amount of fill in them is negligible.

You don't want a locking zipper on a sleeping bag, but if you don't have a locking zipper, the thing will unzip as you thrash around at night. The well-made bag will have a Velcro tab arrangement that can be fastened to prevent this; yet it still enables you to charge out of your sack quickly when an animal investigates your gear at three in the morning. Look for a tab.

Now look at the lower end of the zipper, down by the foot of the bag. This is a designer's nightmare. If he wants the zipper to separate, he has to gusset this area so there's room to separate the beast. But if he gussets it, he leaves a cold spot at the zipper foot, close by your tender little feet. If he's done it right, the draft flap will back this area and will run right down into the foot of the bag. If he's cut corners, there's a little hole there for cold air to find. To close this area properly costs a lot more than it does to do a half-baked job. In fact, one very competent designer tells me that this little nicety adds about five dollars to the manufacturing cost of the bag alone.

While we're down there at the foot, let's take a look at that area in more detail. The typical square-cut looks (and feels) like a bed with a sheet made up smartly at the foot. You have lateral wiggling room, but you can't comfortably lie on your back with your toes uplifted to the heavens unless your feet are a lot smaller than mine. The cheaper mummy bags are built with a variation of this closure. It looks so much like an envelope that it's called that. An envelope foot. It's confining and cold, because you can push your feet against the bottom and push the down aside around your feet. Pretty soon, you have only two layers of nylon, eighteen sullen down-pods, and one feather between you and the Great Outdoors.

This isn't enough. A modification of the envelope puts a down pillow in the foot and sews the sides of the bag to it. That's better. But the really good bags are arranged so that there's room to wiggle your feet — there's extra insulation down there. And the end of the bag is cut in such a way that no matter how hard you push on it, you can't push through to the outer layer of fabric. This, again, is hellishly expensive in terms of manufacturing time; so you pay for dependably warm feet and the room to wiggle them.

There's more you can tell from the outside of a bag, which is going to lead us into that maze which lives between the nylon shells. See those seams running across the top of the bag? They're there to provide little compartments for the down to live in. Down's wiggly stuff, so you have to keep it in smallish tubes for it to stay together. The cheapest bags compartment the down by simply sewing the top shell directly to the inner shell. It's called, understandably enough, *sewn-through construction.* Forget it! Take a look at the cross-section.

COLD AIR

Cold air finds that seam, and oozes on in to say "howdy". It finds more than the seam, because the down doesn't go right up to the seam. It falls away into the center of the tube, so the cold air channel's even larger than it might appear. While a sewn-through sleeper has some application as a liner for another bag for winter use, it generally isn't worth your time to investigate.

What you're far more likely to find at your outfitter's are variations on the basic *box construction,* sometimes called *I-beam.* It looks like this in cross-section:

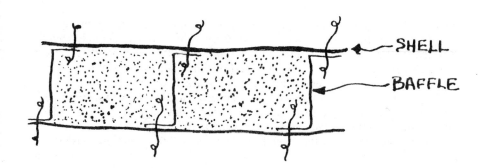

SHELL

BAFFLE

You'll notice that there aren't any sewn-through seams to let the warm out and the cold in. A box construction sleeper doesn't necessarily mean that it's really good. You have to consider a few more things, and for one, you're completely dependent on the integrity of your outfitter. The first and obvious is the width of the tubes. The wider the tubes, the less well the down is controlled and the fewer tubes you have to sew. A tube width of about 8 inches is as wide as you can go with any assurance of relative freedom from cold spots due to shifting of down. Six inches is about standard for a good bag. There's a difference in price. A 72-inch long bag would have twelve 6-inch compartments (ten baffles), while the same bag sewn in 8 inch tubes would have only nine compartments, and seven baffles. That's a difference of six baffles per bag (three on a side). To sew these additional tubes, you need baffling material (almost a third more), additional cutting time, the additional manufacturing time to sew twelve seams, and the additional time in the filling room to weigh the down and fill these extra tubes. That's why you'll pay more for the narrower tubes.

Another important consideration is the baffle material itself and how it's stitched in place. Look again at the stitching rows. A wide stitch — say 6 or 7 per inch — is easily snagged by stray gromblies on the ground and by your toenails. It's also a big expanse of thread to abrade. Too fine a stitch — 12 to 14 per inch — comes perilously close to self-destruction. There's just too many holes too close together for the fabric to hold up well. Eight to ten stitches per inch is optimum. One manufacturer, Sierra Designs, does a fancy hidden stitch to protect this important area from damage. It looks like this:

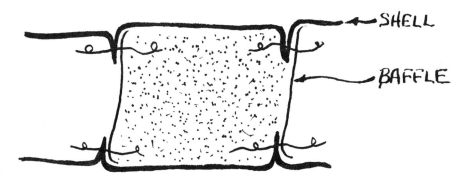

It goes without saying that this type of fussy, meticulous work costs money.

Let's look inside the bag at this baffle material. There are several kinds, cheapest of which is a plain nylon marquisette. Next up the line is a nylon net that is stretchy in one direction and very durable. Strongest of all is a non-directional polyester material which is stretchy, and being a circular weave, holds stitching very well indeed. It's heavier than net, though. One company, Holubar, uses a superlight, 0.9 ounce ripstop as baffling in their best bags. I don't think anybody's ever failed a baffle in one, although it impresses me as overkill. Baffle material doesn't fail, even the cheapest net, except at the stitch line. This may fail for several reasons. If you're building a bag for the junk trade, you use a cheap net which you cut with an electric knife. You don't want to use any extra material so you stitch it very close to the edge. Net's like screening. Pull on it if it's tacked very close to the edge, and it fails. Set the tack in about 10 strands deep, and it's very difficult to pull out. The schlock bag maker catches his big, sloppy stitches about 3 rows back from an unsealed edge in cheap netting, and it tears out. The guy who's building a better bag uses more material, and takes his stitches back 3/4 of an inch or more   He may even roll the baffle, so he's sewing through it twice.

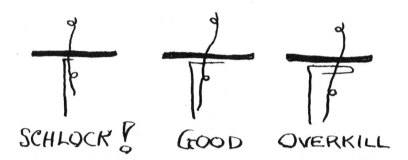

SCHLOCK !   GOOD   OVERKILL

It isn't necessary to do it that way. The stretch net and the omnidirectional fabric hold perfectly well with a single row of stitching, but it's a nice additional fillip if you want to pay the extra machine time to do it.

You don't know what's inside that bag you're looking at? Your outfitter does — or he should. Some people, notably Sierra Designs and Camp 7, provide their dealers with sample baffles, so you can see how their bags are built, and of what. They make good gear — maybe the best anywhere. They have nothing to hide.

There's another type of box construction called the *slant box,* and it looks like this:

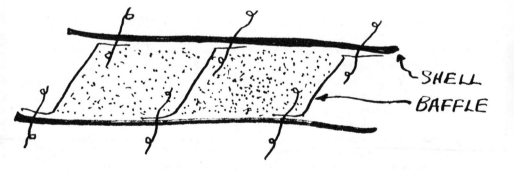

SHELL

BAFFLE

You'll usually find it on the more costly bags, because it takes more baffle material. Lots more. An I-beam bag with 3 inches of loft on a side (6 inches overall) has a baffle that's maybe 4 inches wide to allow the 3 inch loft plus extra to catch the netting securely. The same 3-inch thick bag with a slant box requires a baffle that's closer to 6 inches wide. For twenty baffles, that's over a yard more of material —

of $2.50 a yard material. The theory behind the slant box is that it provides for fuller expansion of the down by accordioning out. This point I find a bit moot. However, the slant wall configuration does provide some support for the down, in that the narrow bottom wedge of one compartment supports the narrow top wedge of its neighbor. Also, down likes to grab onto netting; so the wider net simply keeps more down next to it. It doesn't fall away as easily from the baffle, which helps to maintain loft. This is a small factor, doubtless, but one of those little things that makes the difference between a primo bag and an average one.

There's another kind of baffle that you should know about, but you don't need unless you're headed for a winter traverse of the Presidentials. That's the *double-V tube,* sometimes called the *overlapping tube.* It looks like this:

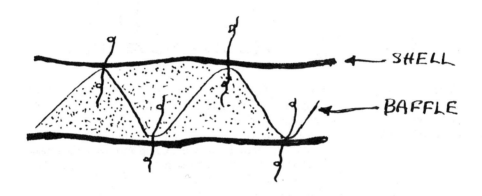

A lot of material is used, and it's a true flaming horror to sew, but it's considered the best means of controlling great masses of down in super-thick winter bags. My own winter sack's built that way, and I haven't been uncomfortable in it at pretty low temperatures and high elevations. But we're not talking winter here. That's a world of its own. So we'll walk on by the double-V sleeper, admiring it on the way and go on to investigate a few other hidden things.

How, by the way, do you tell a slant box bag from a double-V bag? Well, you could read the label and instructions. Or you can simply grab an outside seam with one hand and an inside seam across from it with the other and tug gently, like a kitten worrying a yarn ball. The tug is transmitted to both hands, right? Now to go the inside seam on the other side of the upper seam and tug again. If you can feel the pull, on both hands, it's a double-V. Simple. The topside baffle stitching and the inside stitching will be lined up in a straightforward I-beam bag.

See that seam on the side of the bag opposite the zipper? It's an important seam, because it represents a major potential heat loss if it's done poorly.

The cheapest bags are simply built in two parts, top and bottom, and are sewn together at that side.

Doesn't this look like a sewn-through seam? You bet! And the cold goes marching in — Glory, Glory, Hallelujah! The next upgrading, common in moderate-priced bags and most square-cuts, is the continuous tube:

The shell inners and outers are joined, and the down is free to migrate from the top of the bag to the bottom. This isn't always a detriment, in that you can shake the down from the top to the bottom for warm nights, and from bottom to top on cold ones. The problem is that the down doesn't always want to stay put; so you wind up with cold spots. On a square-cut, you almost have to go that way to maintain uniform loft if the bag is opened up quilt-fashion to be zipped to a mating bag. The optimum method of building a down bag is to provide a barrier at that point to prohibit down shifting, yet enable you to maintain adequate thickness. This device is called a *cross-block* or a *cross-block baffle,* which looks like this:

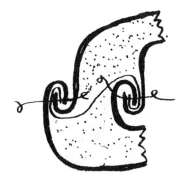

It's simply a piece of baffle material sewn into both seams. In the best bags, the tube baffles are sewn to the cross-block to further prohibit down migration from tube to tube. You need a custom sewing machine for that operation, something called a long-arm bar tacker, and they're not cheap. The process is time-consuming and costs you bread.

Not all cross-blocks are equal. The optimum is the full tube depth cross-block with the tube baffles bar-tacked to it. Yet you probably don't need that fine a bag unless you're planning on using it hard. You do want to check, however, if the baffle really provides a useful thickness of insulation. It's never going to be exactly as thick as the rest of the bag because you have too many seams there that inhibit loft, but it should be pretty thick and uniformly thick as well. The latter point is where you'll find a great difference between the first-rate bags and the rest.

Now let's look at how this seam is made. There's a lot of material here to pull together. There's an upper and lower outer shell, an upper and lower inner shell, a cross-block, and baffle tubes. Let's assume we're not going to bar-tack the baffles to the cross-block for sake of simplicity. So, we have to join the outer shells and the cross-block's outer edge first. We do it like this, so the cross-block is neatly inserted in the middle of a felled seam, and won't pull out.

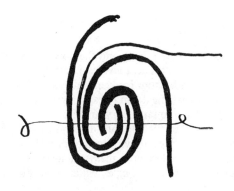

Next we do the same with the inner upper and lower shells, and the inner side of the cross-block. You can do this several ways, but the most straightforward is this way:

You run this seam on a high-speed overcast machine that results in a so-called surged seam, in which the thread actually goes over the top of the material. Think of it as a very long button-hole stitch. Sometimes the upper shell (or the lower if you cut it that way) isn't flipped over, but simply sewn straight.

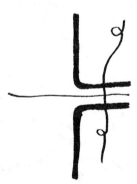

The result is a shade less durable, and a shade less comfortable. Some makers catch the seam in this fashion with one pass, and fell it and restitch it with a cap which makes the seam quite comfortable. Some people even surge the seam and **then** cap it, but this is the solid-gold way to fly, let me tell you. Any of these methods will work. It's obvious that the more complex ones are stronger and more luxurious, but also more expensive. You won't find felled and taped seams on a $65 sleeping bag, and you shouldn't find a plain surged seam on a superbag. You're paying for more than that.

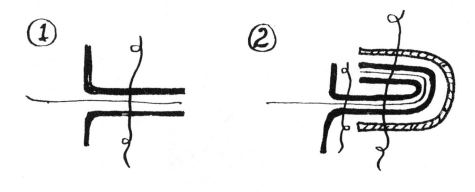

Now let's look into the cutting of the bag. Commonest is the contour cut, in which the inner and outer shells are about the same size. A bag made this way will slump around you and conform to your body, nicely filling all the air spaces. Unfortunately, you can put your butt, or elbow, or knee, or foot against the bag and push the inner shell against the outer shell, displacing the down in between. As I've said before, this leaves but two layers of nylon between you and the Great Outdoors. The superbags use a differential cut, in which the outer shell pattern is significantly wider than the inner shell. This means that when you push a bony protuberance against it, you won't displace the insulation. You gain this at the sacrifice of some of that neat, cozy, "swimming in down" feeling that the contour bags give you.

DIFFERENTIALLY CUT BAG

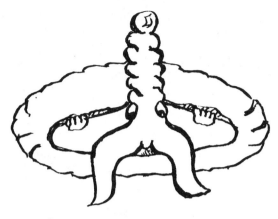

CONTOUR CUT BAG

I confess to preferring a differential cut, but Holubar, for example, prefers the contour cut, and Gerry Cunningham, who still rates with me as the single most innovative designer of outdoor gear and a man whose gear created the backpacking revolution, always championed it. On the other hand, very able dudes like George Lamb of Camp 7, Harry Hunt at Alpine Designs, George Marks and Bob Swanson at Sierra Designs and Justus Bauschinger of Class 5 feel that the differentially-cut bag offers optimum insulation.

In general, your best bags in a quality manufacturer's line are differentially cut. It's a little tougher to sew, as you have to gather your baffles as you sew them in, or contour-cut them like Camp 7 does, and you have separate patterns for the inner and outer shells. This means another cutting operation. As we know by now, any extra time on a sewing machine or a cutting table costs the manufacturer money. And if it costs them money, it costs you money. Even so, if I was in the market for another down bag, I'd buy a differentially cut bag.

Now that you're clued in on what's inside a sleeping bag beside down, and what to look for outside that tips you off on what's inside, let's look at a couple of little finishing details that you should be aware of – the hood, or if you *really* want a square cut, the shoulder drawstrings. Do they work? Or has some being sewed the drawcords into the seam in a few places? Don't laugh. You wouldn't believe how many I've seen! It works? Great. Do the drawcords have either leather dingbats on them or cord locks to keep them where you want them? Fine. You can add these fillips if they're not there. The leather's pleasanter against your skin; the plastic cord locks work better. Your choice.

Of more import is the drawhem itself. That's the little cloth tunnel the cord runs through. Doubled fabric is really good construction. Nylon is easily abraded; nylon loveth not abrasion, so seek out a two-layer drawhem, hemmed at the ends so you're not tugging on raw fabric, and sewn in such a way that you won't tear out the whole works if you give it a sharp tug.

The drawcord itself? A flimsy, already frayed masterpiece, or is it instead a good, solid overlong bootlace of flat cordura braid? Make sure it's substantial to to begin with. You should even check out the stuff bag that comes with it to see if the drawcord works, although I've generally used the stuff bags that came with my two bags for other purposes and bought a large-size Sierra West stuff bag.

This is a lot of material to digest in one sitting. Here's a shifty little table that tells you what you can expect in terms of construction details and designs in down bags in that 15-25 degree range.

PRICE RANGE

	HIGH	MODERATE	LOW	SCHLOCK
Zipper	#10 YKK, Opta Coil, Talon Ladder	#7 YKK	#5 YKK; YKK or Talon coil	coil or metal
Type:	Double bug separating	Double bug separating	Non-separating	Non-separating
Tube Baffles:	6-in. slant box	8-in. I beam	10-in. I beam	12-in. I-beam (rarely) or sewn-through
Baffle Material:	Stretch net or omniweave	Stretch net or omniweave	Net	Marquisette if I-beam
Crossblock:	full-width, bar tacked	crossblock not tacked	no cross-block	sewn-through
Draft tube:	full-length, very gener-ous; not sewn through	generous; not sewn through	skimpy but suitable; sewn through	sewn through if present at all
Shell Material:	1.9 ripstop, downproof	1.9 ripstop, downproof	2.2 taffeta	whatever being closed out, usually taffeta seconds, if you're lucky.
Filling :	prime goose	good goose or prime duck	serviceable duck or goose duck blend	"waterfowl down and feathers" which means just about what you want it to mean
Foot:	baffled differential cut	baffled	envelope or "pillow"	envelope
Cut:	differential	differential	contour	contour

I have the luxury of a huge old farmhouse with lots of space to hang up my bags and air them out. Most people don't have that kind of closet room. If you don't, either buy a huge storage bag of breatheable cotton/polyester fabric at your outfitter's (Camp 7 and Class 5 both make them) or make something like it out of an old sheet or two old pillowcases. The bag will stay in there happily, well aired and not crushed in an amorphous, damp little lump in a stuffy corner. You simply cannot store a damp down bag in its stuff sack! It will rot. In fact, owning a down bag requires that you know a few things about cleaning it. If the shell is dirty, it can be sponged with mild soap and water and dried at either "delicate fabric" setting or preferably no heat in a home dryer. Be careful! The home dryer is pretty small, and a bag is big. Even on "delicate fabric", check it out regularly. Avoid the big commercial dryers. They're the right size for a bag, but too hot, and you'll go through dimes like you were in the Greyhound station in Reno before you'll dry a sleeping bag in one of them.

If the bag is really scrofulous, it should be cleaned to remove excess oils from the down, to say nothing of removing your foxy odor. You can wash a down bag. *Mild* detergent (Woolite works well) and lukewarm water and a bathtub. Get right in there with it! You really have to wrestle the thing to submerge it! Then slosh it around good for a while and rinse until you're tired of rinsing – then rinse again. Gather it up in your arms, all in a bunch, and squeeze. Squeeze about like you'd hug a kid, not like you'd hug a consenting adult, as the phrase goes. Don't pick the bag out of the water by grabbing a piece and hoisting the poor thing unceremoniously out of the water by one corner. Get right down there and wallow in the tub! After the bag has drained all it seems to want to, take the sodden mess to your dryer, and let it spin around for the rest of the day at "delicate fabric". If you're lucky, this will dry it enough so you can make an attempt to redistribute the lumps of down to enhance further drying. Then it's back in the dryer again. Ultimately, it's good to hang the thing outside on a nice sunny day for the last fine touch of drying. I don't suppose it really matters, but the bag comes out smelling better for the sunlight.

If this sounds like a hassle, it's supposed to. If you're lucky, you can find a dry cleaner in your area who knows how to work with down. What you're looking for is a cleaner who uses Stoddard's solvent or some other mild **petroleum base solvent**, and uses a big, low temperature, high air volume dryer. There aren't many. The usual dry cleaning solvent, perchlorethylene, strips too much oil from the bag.

POLYESTER SLEEPERS

If you're not up to laying out the dollars for a good down bag, or if you're unwilling to go to the hassle of keeping the bag healthy and happy, or if the idea of an insulation that's warm when wet turns you on, look closely at the polyester bags. In fact, look at them anyway, even if you think you'd prefer a downie, because they're good enough to constitute a valid alternative. The construction methods aren't as complex, so evaluation's a lot more straightforward.

The differences between Polarguard and Fiberfill II require different construction techniques. Let's look at Polarguard first, because it's a simpler material to handle from a manufacturer's viewpoint.

Polarguard, as you remember, is a continuous filament fiberfill, and it comes as batting in different thicknesses. As it's pretty tough stuff, and stoutly resists separation when it's pummeled, pounced on, and poked by protuberances, an acceptable sleeper can be made by simply stitching the shell to the batting around the edges. The more sophisticated builder will use two layers of batting, and stitch the upper layer to the outer shell and the lower layer to the inner shell at the periphery.

The ends will then be joined by the upper and lower zipper halves, and a draft tube sewn in. Again, the better practice is to sew the draft tube to the inner shell rather than sew it through both shells. Another good way is simply to attach the zipper part way up the outer shell, making the bag itself a draft tube.

Some folks use a three-layer construction, in which the upper insulation bat is stitched to the outer shell, the lower bat to the inner shell, and the middle bat is stitched only at the edges. This gives you a bag that looks like our old friend the slant box. This is a more elaborate, and more costly, method than is required for a three-season Polarguard bag, but I've seen a couple of dandy ten below zero Polarguard sleepers built this way. Don't assume that every synthetic sack that has those distinctive transverse stitch patterns like a down bag is a three-layer Polarguard, or even a two-layer. Watch out for bags on the market where the stitching is simply decoration! Pass them by, no matter how good they may be otherwise.

Fiberfill II, being a chopped fiber, requires more control than Polarguard. It hangs together better than down, to be sure, but it isn't really a batting, either. Probably the best technique for handling it is North Face's, in which the material is shingled, as it were. If you were to split a North Face Fiberfill II bag lengthwise down the middle, the top layer would look like this:

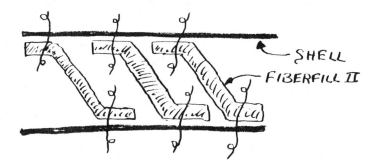

That's a lot of sewing, but it works. Beware of any Fiberfill II that's merely stitched around the periphery of the bag. The insulation will separate, and the bag will develop cold spots. Fiberfill II in the flesh comes much closer to down in respect to "feel" than its rival Polarguard, but it still feels plastic when sewn in a sleeper. This leads me to conclude that we haven't hit on an optimum design and sewing method for Fiberfill II bags thus far.

As far as evaluating workmanship in a Fiberfill II bag, there isn't anything I can tell you that we haven't already covered elsewhere, except to remind you again that peripherally-sewn Fiberfill II will separate and develop cold spots.

7. INTO AND ONTO THE GREAT OUTDOORS

*"make me a pallet
down on your floor . . ."*
American folk song

The best sleeping bag in the world, and the snuggest, driest tent will not combine to insure you a good night's sack time if you've picked a bummer of a campsite.

First on the obvious list is to select a site with a reasonable proximity to, but not in, water. Fetching drinking water from a sparkling little rill is neat to do, but not when it's a half-mile uphill.

Far worse than a dry camp is a camp where you can fill your canteen from the water in your tent. Water flows downhill; but from the number of poor souls I see every year setting up in a little hollow that just fits their tent, it's apparently one physical phenomenon that has avoided the public gaze. If you're steeped in Old Woodsmen-type lore, you're going to tell me to ditch the tent so the water runs off. Well, I'm as steeped as the next, but I don't ditch my tent because I want to leave the terrain as I found it, without neat little embryo gullies all over the landscape. Look for a little local high spot, and simply avoid the neat little depressions that look so cozy.

A small, fetid pool in your tent is a bummer, but water flowing through it is some sort of ultimate anguish. There's always somebody who decides that *the* place to make camp is on that lovely sandbar alongside that lovely stream – gurgle, gurgle. Suddenly during the night a thunderstorm dumps an inch of rain on a nearby mountain in fifteen minutes, while you sit in your tent commenting on the fantastic display down the trail a mile or so, and congratulate yourself on your good fortune. Not a drop here! You roll over and drop off in the light of the waning lightning.

A half-hour later you're wriggled awake by two six-inch brook trout flopping in your sleeping bag and a half-grown muskrat holding onto your left ear. Congratulations! You have just learned that when water flows downhill after a rain, it's all gotta go somewhere. In the East, much of it is absorbed in the deep forest duff. But a heavy rain brings heavy runoff, and streams rise fast. This isn't that terrifying spectacle you get in the West, where a ten-foot deep crest can come howling down a dry wash, leaving death and destruction in its wake. The Eastern forest soils are too absorbent for that to happen. But I have seen Calamity Brook run over its banks to fill a lot of ill-pitched tents with six inches of cold, moving water after a hard rain. Avoid this by making camp well above the level of any nearby stream.

87

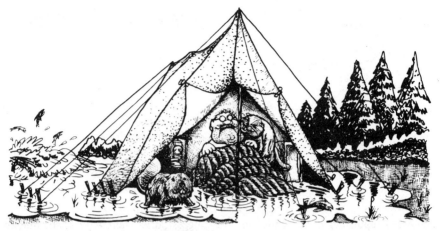

While good site selection is certainly a key to a comfortable night in the boon-docks, the most important item is whatever goes under your sleeping bag. No, that gorgeous, expensive nylon and goose down confection isn't enough to keep you warm. Any insulation that's compressible enough to be used for backpacking will compress under your weight. In the case of a down bag, it will compress to next to nothing under your hips and shoulders. The polyester bags are a little better, but only a little. So, you need something under your sleeping bag to provide insulation, and in the process, a moisture barrier. You have three choices: an air mattress, a closed-cell foam pad, or an open-cell foam pad. Let's look at them in that order.

The air mattress has been with us for many, many years, beginning its long and checkered career as a pneumatic bed. It's been heavy and cumbersome, prone to leaks, and requires lungs like a sulphur-bottomed whale to inflate. But the times they are a-changin! Today a good backpacking air mattress is a tough, light con-trivance, and well worth considering for comfort. Probably the most comfortable air mattress is the I-beam type, which gives you a relatively flat surface, but is also heavy and expensive. The cheaper air mattress, which is a row of tubes heat-sealed together, is a bit lighter, less comfortable, and generally not made for the rigors of backpacking. What you want, then is a rubberized nylon mattress (not cotton, and definitely not plastic), built in an I-beam configuration. A full-length (72 inches) mattress is the epitome of comfort — and weighs close to 4 pounds. A three-footer will do the job nicely at half the weight. Sure, your feet hang off, but the heavy parts of your body are well supported. Your clothes go under your feet.

There's another breed of air mattress around that I've had occasion to use a few times. It's called the Air-Lift, and I suppose you'd have to think of it as a second-generation air bed. This is a nylon shell, zippered on one end, and filled with sturdy plastic tubes. "Sturdy" is the word. Flotation bags for white-water boats are made out of the same material. Each tube has its own valve, and can be filled with one good breath. Each tube can be removed, and replaced if necessary. In fact, they give you a spare tube! The whole bit weighs less than a pound and a half in 36-inch length. I've almost converted back to an air mattress.

But air mattresses, no matter how good, are still subject to failure and are cold. That isn't dead air in there — it's air that's constantly circulating every time you move. And that circulating air spirits heat away from your body.

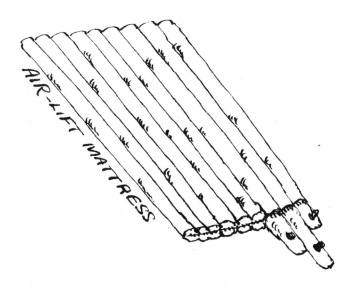

Far more reliable, much warmer, and frankly less comfortable is the closed-cell foam pad, of which the best known and most widely available is Ensolite. This is an admirable material, really. It's tough and absorbs no water due to its closed cell structure; insulation properties are excellent, and it's self-extinguishing in case you're careless enough to set it on fire. Comfortable it ain't. Ensolite is made in 84-inch square sheets, which tends to limit the available sizes. Commonest are 21″ x 42″ and 18½″ x 63″. It's available also in quarter inch, three-eighths, and half inch thicknesses. The thinnest is acceptable for warmth, certainly, but offers no comfort whatever. The 3/8-inch is a good compromise to my way of thinking, and I use a 3/8 inch pad that's 63 inches long for everything but winter work.

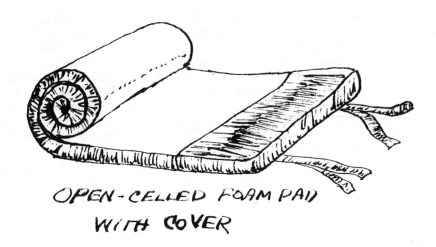

OPEN-CELLED FOAM PAD
WITH COVER

You want the white Ensolite, the so-called Type M. A green Ensolite, which is a little denser and more flexible in extreme cold, is available for the winter mountaineer. It's also significantly more expensive. You don't need it.

Ensolite isn't the only closed cell foam available, although it's the commonest. There's a much lighter foam around – a waxy-feeling, dense, easily torn substance that is distributed through several sources. And this form usually doesn't bear a brand name unless it comes from Daley Foam Products, which calls it O-So-Lite. They're O-So-Rite. This foam also supports combustion, which spooks some people, although I confess that it doesn't bother me. The foam's not too comfortable, but cheap, light, waterproof, and warm. If you're limited in bucks, consider it. Folks call it "funny foam" in a lot of shops, so you could ask for it by that name.

By far the commonest foam pad is the open-celled variety. Open-celled foam is essentially a sponge, and is remarkably thirsty stuff, which has to be covered with a coated nylon fabric to keep it dry. The best pads have one side covered with a breatheable polyester/cotton or brushed nylon so your sleeping bag doesn't skate off them and can breathe a little. The open-cell pads usually come in one and a half inch thickness. They're plenty comfortable, if a bit bulky. They're compressible, though, and a 72 incher can be rolled up to a diameter of 9 inches. The pads come in various lengths, typically 36, 42, 48 and 72 inches long, and are usually between 18 and 22 inches wide.

A few words are in order about the selection of open-celled pads. First, select a firm one. It'll last longer and be more comfortable. Next, select one that has one side done in uncoated fabric. Then make sure that the tie tapes are sewn firmly onto the shell. Beyond that, there isn't anything to be wary about. This is a pretty simple piece of gear.

Using your sleeping pad properly, be it air mattress or foam, is rather obvious. Try to avoid bedding down on rocks, stumps and roots. If you're in a sandy area, lie down on your pad and wriggle around a bit to rearrange a little depression for your hips. Don't, however, chop up the forest duff for this. Finally, arrange your bed so that your head is level with or slightly above your feet. Sleeping with your head down, even slightly, is most unpleasant.

I have my own ritual. Not that you should necessarily follow it, but it works for me. After I've pitched my tent (or tarp), I pull the sleeping bag out of its stuff sack and either lay it out in the tent or hang it over a branch to fluff up. I use my Ensolite pad as a camp chair; so that stays with me. At bedtime, my clothes go under my feet (or in my pack, if I'm using a tarp) my socks go in my boots, as do my glasses, and my down jacket goes in the sleeping bag stuff sack to be used as a pillow. Then I crawl into the sack, and after it gets warmed up, I roll over on my belly, prop myself up on my elbows and do a few whiffs of my pipe as I watch the night settle around me. The pipe goes into my boots, and I retreat all the way into my sack and go to sleep.

8. EAT RIGHT WITHOUT HASSLES

"Oh them beans, bacon 'n' gravy
They almost drive me crazy. . ."
— Depression folk song

I have a friend who lives on Wilson's meat bars, sugar cubes, powdered milk and dried apricots when he goes into the boonies. Needless to say, he doesn't need to worry about cooking gear beyond a cup, and he doesn't have to hassle sources of heat. Most of us ordinary mortals wouldn't relish a diet of that sort for too long. This doesn't mean that you have to truck along a *cordon bleu* chef with his *batterie de cuisine* and three different kinds of stock on the top bar of your pack. What you want is simply prepared, nourishing fare in large quantities. I believe in eating what you like to eat.

Backpacking can be a stress situation for many people — genuinely physical work, coupled with the emotional shifting of gears that you have to make to cope with an unfamiliar environment. How odd to consider the natural world as an unfamiliar environment. The problem is compounded by family backpacking, which typically throws the male into a situation that he's ill-prepared to cope with — especially if his wife is even less prepared than he is for the cultural transition. Kids, being cheerful little savages that they are, adapt splendidly. They hate to be chained up for eight hours a day anywhere.

Why compound this shock by being forced to munch on flat-tasting swill? If you like spaghetti, do it. Yep, it's available freeze-dried, although pasta is an eminently transportable food. Like shrimp creole? Franks and beans? Beef stew? Take them. They too are available in freeze-dried form. If I harp on freeze-dried foods, it's simply because they're great weight-savers. A can of good old Dinty Moore's beef stew weighs a couple of pounds plus. Freeze-dried stew that makes up to the same amount maybe weighs ten ounces. You don't have a cruddy can to stomp flat and carry out with you, either. To give you an idea of what's available in freeze-dried and dehydrated foods, here's a specimen list of offerings from two major processors, Rich Moor and Oregon Freeze Dried Foods (Mountain House). Don't accept this partial list as gospel, because both houses drop slow-moving items and add new items constantly. Add to the list the extensive array of goodies you can get at your friendly local supermarket, and you should be able to surround yourself with familiar, palatable, easily prepared and easily carried foods.

LIST OF GOODIES AVAILABLE

Main Courses	Meats	Desserts
Beef Stew	Bacon Bar	Chocolate Cream Pie
Chicken Stew	Pork Chops	Lemon Pie
Beef and Rice	Hamburger	Raspberry Cobbler
Beef Stroganoff	Meatballs	Blueberry Cobbler
Shrimp Creole	Sausage Patties	Pineapple Cheesecake
Chile Con Carne		French Apple Compote
Beef Chop Suey	**Vegetables**	Banana Cream Pie
Chicken Chop Suey		
Chicken Pilaf	Peas	
Chili Mac	Corn	
Macaroni and Cheese	Green Beans	
Spaghetti and Meatballs	Carrots	
Chicken Romanoff		
Chicken à la King		
Spanish Rice		
Lasagna		

Now you have to find something to cook this chow in. You remember all those cooksets at your outfitters? Those cunningly nested pots and kettles and lids that turn into frying pans? Now that you remember them, forget them for the most part, unless you're backpacking with a considerable tribe that likes full-course dinners.

I use two pots that nest inside each other. They're of a fairly generous size, one and a half quart and one quart. The larger will cook a one-pot dinner for four people. The smaller one heats water for tea or coffee, or makes a dessert. Each party member carries his own stainless steel cup, the kind that's acquired the generic name of Sierra Cup, and a tablespoon. You eat out of the cup — or you simply dip into the pot. Plates? You don't need plates. You're not out there to wash dishes! Frying pan? You can do most foods, including scrambled eggs, in a pot. If you're into fishing, a fry pan may be useful — but a trout skewered on a green stick and grilled isn't half bad, and you don't have a pan to clean afterward.

SIGG NESTING POTS

By the way, if you're really into the recycling trip, you can fashion your own pots and it won't cost you a nickel. Just find yourself a big juice can (46 ounce), a one pound coffee can and a squatty little 12-ounce can like Mexicorn comes in. Soak off the labels, smooth off the opened edge with a file, mark the little can in 2-ounce increments and wrap its top with tape, and you have a usable, although not terribly durable, cookset and cup. To finish it off to the queen's taste, add a backpacker's pot gripper to the kit, and set up a wire bail handle for the 46-ounce can so you can use it more easily as a water bucket. You're in business! Some aluminum foil will serve as a pot lid.

RECYCLED COOKWARE,
PROVEN THE LENGTH
AND BREADTH OF THE U.S.A.

If you don't want to go this route, select a few pots from your outfitter that nest, keeping in mind a few ground rules.

1. The so-called "scout kits" and the cheapie aluminum kits with the screw-on handles are unmitigated trash, unsuitable for backyard camping.
2. Good nesting pots with lids aren't cheap. The Sigg or Trangia pots, which I think are the best available, are hellishly expensive, but very durable, and their slightly rounded bottom corners make them easy to clean. There are also some good English and German pots available under a wide variety of trade names depending on who imports them. *Buy something sturdy even if it costs a bit more and weighs a bit more.*
3. A pot that's unstable, or that can't be gripped securely with a pot gripper is less than useless. Try all pots out on your preferred heat source to see if they're compatible. If they're not, walk on, brother. A bootful of beef stew is damn poor fare for a hungry backpacker.

So much for pots, except to comment on their maintenance. Botulism is such an ugly word! So is that common ailment known variously as the G.I.'s, Montezuma's Revenge, or the trots. Clean your pots and utensils. I carry a small green scouring pad and a tube of Trak biodegradable soap in a Ziploc bag just for such uses. Camp-suds or Sutter's are also good soaps for this, but I avoid the household detergents because they don't break down readily. Scrub in *hot* water, rinse thoroughly, and don't throw the rinsewater in the creek! Don't scrub the bottom of the pots. Leave them black. They're more efficient heat-holders that way. Just carry them in a stuff sack so you don't schmutz up your old lady's sweater.

Now to heat sources. You'll notice that I haven't mentioned cooking fires, except for grilling trout, and I don't intend to go into a long rap about cooking fires because I feel that they're ethically indefensible in heavily-used areas. Furthermore, in many areas, they're prohibited for several good reasons. Forest fires are the most obvious.

The second is a bit more subtle, and you have to see it to appreciate it. Let's set up a little scenario. Adirondack Mountains, four o'clock in the afternoon. You've just taken a leisurely walk up from Tahawus over Indian Pass, and you've taken the time to gawk at the stupendous thousand-foot headwall of Wallface. You've poked around the giant shoulders and made snowballs on this 90-degree day from the per-petual snowpack beneath them. Then it's over the pass and down to Scott's Clear-ing. A delightful place, Scott's. The ruins of an old logging dam there, even a few odd bits of scrap from the old days of logging. Not wilderness, really, but an excel-lent tent site with open shade, good water and a delicious view of the Pass. And seventy years of time has mellowed the presence of the loggers. The forests have won. What's left of man's brief incursion is more a source of interest than of grief. Or is it? Look at the trees! They're scalped up to eight feet off the ground. And those saplings. My God, they're chewed off a foot above ground! The poor, spindly stumps catch your boots and send you sprawling. Every twenty feet there's the curdled, half-charred remnant of somebody's cooking fire, adorned with un-burned polybags and unburnable aluminum foil. The place looks like the morning after Shiloh; all because a large number of jackasses didn't give a damn about the environment or what the next guy would find.

Now it's easy to build a cooking fire in some areas in a fashion that leaves no trace. There may be a time when you have to. Stoves have been known to fail, or to be forgotten. We'll get to that in another chapter. Let's just say that your pri-mary heat source for cooking is a stove.

While there's a broad selection of backpacking stoves on the market, I'm going to climb way out on a most slender limb and recommend that you consider only two stoves – the Optimus 8R and the Svea 123. They're widely sold; parts are readily available; and they're rugged; light, dependable, and use a readily procurable fuel. There are other good gasoline-fired stoves on the market beside the 8R and the 123, to be sure.

The big, burly blowtorch-in-a-box Optimus 111B is the standard winter traveler's stove, but you don't need this 56-ounce moose for summer backpacking. The Enders Benzin Baby, a German stove, is a fine performer, but its price is about to go out of sight and its distribution is charmingly erratic. You may wind up with a stove ren-dered useless for want of an unobtainable 25 cent fuel nozzle. The Phoebus stoves seem to work well, but again, parts are hard to get.

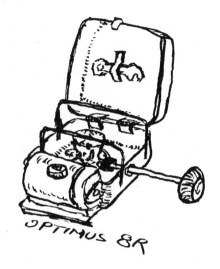

OPTIMUS 8R

SVEA 123
WITHOUT WINDSCREEN

Coleman has the technology to make a great stove. Their old G.I. stoves were tremendous, although heavy, but their current offering, the Sportster, is dramatically overweight and oversized and underpowered. Larry Penberthy, the flinty old wood-chuck in charge of Mountain Safety Research, makes a great expedition stove, but it throttles down poorly and is a fussier unit than the occasional hiker will want. Also, you can't generally go to your nearest shop and get parts for the beast. I hate to lay a bum rap on the MSR stove, because it's really a fine performer. But it's simply not a great stove for the average dude.

There's a host of small LP-gas stoves kicking around, and they're popular. They're certainly light, and anyone can use them. I like the Primus Mousetrap pretty well, and I like the design theories behind Gerry Mini Mark II and the Richmoor Alp, but none of them have the heat output of a gasoline stove. All require a special cartridge, although the Richmoor can use either the Bleuet or Primus cartridges. Neat little stoves, but you're still tied to a very specific fuel requirement, and you have empty cartridges to pack out. If you're willing to pack 'em out, by all means go ahead with the LP stove.

By the way, there has been much talk of poor quality control of fittings and cartridges for these LP stoves. I've had the occasion to see a few first hand at my local outfitter's. While you can tinker a gasoline stove in the field, tinkering the LP jobbies is pretty counterproductive. If you really like LP stoves, try yours in the shop to be sure its act is all together.

When you buy your 8R or 123, you need a few more items. Get a spare fuel tank cap, a spare fuel nozzle, and a cleaning needle replacement. Some 123's (designated the 123R) have self-cleaning burners; the plain old 123 doesn't. The 8R is a self-cleaner. The self-cleaners use a needle mounted on the top of a rack up through the nozzle, and the little needles can get bunged up in use. A badly bent needle will interfere with the normal operation of the stove. Carry a spare. Also, get a big eye-dropper from a drugstore, and put this and your spare parts in a little Ziploc bag. Put the whole mess into the stove's stuff sack. The reason for a stuff sack for the stove is to keep it from leaking fuel and/or spilled stew in your pack. Even if you can fit the stove inside your cook kit – and with the Svea it's easy – keep it, and its spare in a sack. The day will come when you'll be glad you did.

So, you're heading home with your new stove. Don't forget fuel and a fuel bottle. Get Coleman fuel. You can use **regular** gasoline in an 8R or a 123 in an emergency, but it will crud up the nozzle in time and the lead fumes will mess up your punkin-haid pretty badly if you use it indoors. Coleman fuel. Not kerosene, turpentine, alcohol, paint thinner, cherry brandy, lighter fluid or diesel fuel. No, I'm not being funny. I've seen stoves come into my shop for repair filled up to the gizzard with these things. Coleman fuel. And a fuel bottle. The commonest is the cylindrical, spun aluminum anodized Sigg bottle, but I prefer a flat tin bottle made by Cavog.

It packs better, pours infinitely better, and seems to be less susceptible to leakage. It's also more expensive. I like the one and a half pint (roughly) size. This is enough for a long weekend, and you'll have a bit left over to help out some poor soul who's spilled his and is really hurting for a hot meal in the middle of one of our rare North-eastern rainstorms.

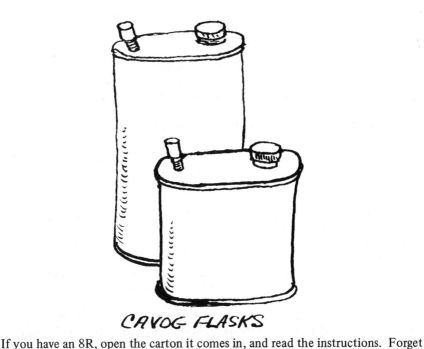

CARVOG FLASKS

If you have an 8R, open the carton it comes in, and read the instructions. Forget their silly "hold in the hand to warm it up" starting procedure. Forever remember this maxim: **never open the fuel cap while the stove is in operation.** Now, open the 8R's little blue box, and slide the beast out. Put the throttle key in place and turn it to the right. That closes the fuel valve. Now turn it to the left, and look through the burner plate at the fuel nozzle. As you turn the handle to the left (counter clockwise, that is) you'll see a little needle rise up magically through the orifice. That's the cleaning needle. This means that fuel throttle on the stove is somewhere between fuel right (off) and fuel left (cleaning). You can kill your stove by turning the knob fuel left while it's operating because you simply are plugging up the fuel orifice. Don't confuse that with turning the stove off, however. Turning the knob to "clean" simply cleans. It doesn't shut off the fuel at the valve body, so if you put the little mucker away that way it will leak, usually through the packing on the stem.

To make the stove run, turn the valve off, and open the tank cap. Fill the beast with Coleman fuel, and try not to fill the box with fuel at the same time. Take your resident eyedropper, suck up a snootful of fuel from the open tank, and squirt this into the spirit cup on the bottom of the burner. Give it another one this time. Some stoves like to be warmed up longer than others, and you may find that yours works with half a dropperful. Close the fuel lid, get your fuel bottle out of the way, light a match, and poke it at the spirit cup. Ignition. If you've dawdled in hot weather, or sloshed fuel into the little blue box, it will ignite with a jolly little "rumph" and singe the hair on the back of your delicate little paddies. Let it burn cheerfully until it's just about out, and crack the valve a little. You should be greeted by a satisfying little roar as the volatized fuel ignites.

If not, close the valve, light a match, poke it through one of the holes in the side of the burner head, and crack the valve again. That should do it. If nothing happens, close the valve, douse the match, and open the valve again. Do you hear a little hissing sound? Okay, perhaps you didn't open the valve enough the first time. Try it again with the match. Keep it at about half throttle for a while, and then turn it up. Play with it. See how far you can open the throttle before the cleaning needle cuts down the flame. See how low you can throttle it without killing it. Play with it and get to know it.

What happens if the little beast doesn't hiss when the valve opens, or it hisses for a second and peters out? Well, these are problems you'll run into in the field sometimes; so before you rush back to your outfitter screaming for a refund, let's try to figure it out.

The 8R (and the 123) run in the following fashion. The preheat cycle (the eyedropper bit) warms up the burner assembly, and volatizes the fuel that's been heretofore soaking up in a wick that runs from the tank into the burner assembly. This builds up a fair head of pressure, which is relieved a bit when the valve is opened. As the stove operates, the heat it generates cooks your chow and continues to warm the valve unit to the point where the fuel in the tank vaporizes a bit. Don't worry. The tank lid is a safety valve. If you build up too much pressure — and about the only way you can do that is to so enclose the stove that it gets no ventilation — the valve will pop, and a rather terrifying spout of flame will erupt from it. Just let it burn out and cool off, and start looking for your spare fuel cap.

This is a closed system. If there's no hiss, there's a leak somewhere in it, or you haven't preheated it enough. Try another application of the eyedropper. If this doesn't produce a hiss and a flame, make sure that the tank lid is on snugly. Also make sure that the valve packing nut is snug, and that the fuel nozzle is tight. You can check this by unscrewing the tulip-shaped burner cup, using the little wrench that Optimus gives you. All snug and still no go? Put on the spare burner cap. That should do it.

The commonest failure mode for the new 8R's and 123's (and Primus 71's and Optimus 111B's too) is a poorly assembled safety valve in the tank cap. Get to know this beast, and it will save you much grief. There are two kinds. One has a slotted top with a little widget sticking up into the slot. That's the old type, and it's the better of the two because you can fix it with a screwdriver. The newer kind requires a special tool, essentially a 5-sided Allen wrench of about 3.5 millimeter size. Maybe you can get one from your outfitter, although chances are he has trouble getting them. If you're patient, you can file an old Allen wrench to fit.

At any rate, once you either unscrew the little slotted head jobbie or unwrench this new contraption, you'll find that they're almost the same. You'll find a plunger with a shoulder on it, and a little neoprene dingbat stuck in the end of it. The plunger is kept in check by a spring that looks like it came from a cheap ballpoint pen. (It doesn't, but you can cut a ballpoint spring and use it if you have to.) The trouble point is that the little dingbat on the end may have been set in cockeyed, so that it doesn't seal. Pummel the little beast a bit and set the thing square. Then it will seal, and the stove will function. If you blow a safety valve, this gadget usually gets fried, and Optimus, damn them, doesn't sell replacements. A little ingenuity here will save the day. Neoprene gasket material will work, as will a glob of RTV silicone rubber. Drop it in place in the plunger end, which is wrapped with tape to build up height, and slice it off at the right height after it cures. So much for technical obsolescense!

Got it squared away and working? Fine and dandy. The other common problem point with the 8R and the 123 is a function of age, and that's erosion of the fuel nozzle so that the fuel isn't volatized properly or is spurted out skeewoggy. The fuel path has to be essentially straight up, where it will strike the burner plate and deflect around it. This is really where combustion takes place. Incidentally, if the burner plate's on cockeyed, the stove won't work well. If you lose the burner plate, you have a gasoline-powered candle, so don't lose the burner plate. That's why we keep the stove in a bag.

The starting procedure with the Svea 123 is similar, with or without the self-cleaning needle. The difference, of course, is that you can't shut the stove down by opening the valve all the way with the standard needle. Other than that, the two beasties are similar. The only hassle with the 123 is that you'll find it easiest to torch off with the windscreen off. This means that you have to pick up a frumious Svea and put its windscreen on while it's running. It's easier than it sounds. Just don't dawdle.

You'll note that the Svea comes with a little tin cup and cup lifter, which you can give to your children with impunity. It also comes with a chain that tethers the control handle to the stem. The chain breaks. Untether it, and hang it from the windscreen if you like it attached. Otherwise, file the thing in your spare parts Ziploc along with your tank lid, fuel nozzle and eyedropper. Attach a short length of bright red shoelace to it so you can find it when you drop it. Not "if," when. Unless you have hands that are absolutely insensitive, you do not keep a Svea control handle on the valve stem when the stove is running. It gets savagely hot.

As to making a choice between the two stoves (and I should include the Primus 71L and Optimus 80, which are tin-can container versions of the 123, but with a bigger fuel tank), it's pretty academic. The Svea is lighter, but a little more of a hassle to use, and a little tippier. The 8R is a super-durable affair, but it won't fit inside most cooksets. Take your choice. The 71L and the 80 are not commonly found. They work, but can also be unstable. I keep coming back to the Svea. I'm willing to live with its inconveniences and have had excellent luck with it. It also fits in my cookset.

Which brings up another point. Sigg makes an excellent cookset with a windscreen unit that's built around the 123, and Optimus makes a much less fancy unit with one pot for the 123. Everything fits into one pot, and it's a nice unit. Expensive, but nice. For that, you must remove the brass windscreen from your 123. The misguided people who simply cut out the Sigg windscreen so the entire 123 would fit, blew up their stoves. Mean time to catastrophic failure based on 11 such incidents in my experience as an outfitter is 8.6 minutes; so be advised.

That's it for stoves and cooking gear. Now let's fix up some supper. With two pots only!

While you're getting your shelter set up, fill both buckets with water and fire up the larger one. Relax, and have a cup of soup or tea or coffee. That'll use some of the water. Fill up the pot again, and stew it up to cook your main dish in. Meanwhile, prepare dessert, if you're into dessert, in the smaller pot. The quickie desserts usually have to set up an hour or so. Brew up the hoosh of your preference, eat some, clean out the pot and the cups, and do up a bit more water for post-prandial coffee. By that time your dessert is done, and you're in fine shape. Eat the dessert out of the communal bowl, and wash it and the spoons with the leftover hot water in the big pot. *Finis!*

To sum it up, you can cook comfortably for several people with the following gear:

Stove, Svea 123 or Optimus 8R
1½ quart pot, covered or coverable with foil
1-quart pot, ditto
potlifter
Sierra cups and tablespoons all around.

Added conveniences are:

1-quart wide-mouth polybottle. Useful for presoaking freeze-dried meats to cut down cooking time, and for shaking up powdered milk or juices.

Six small poly vials or bottles containing salt, pepper, basil, oregano, soy sauce and rosemary. Take more or less as your taste dictates.

A ladle, of French origin, detachable handle.

And a few luxuries:

A teapot, with a tea egg if you're into drinking tea. The teapot is a useful, effective water boiler, and cuts down on the swap-the-pot routine considerably.

A frying pan, folding handle, Teflon coated.

A spatula. If you're into frying, they're handy.

9. FIRE AND THE ZERO IMPACT CAMPSITE

"Only trash make trash."
– USCA decal, seen on racing canoe
at Pine Creek

I said earlier that I view unrestricted use of fire for cooking as morally indefensible in heavily-used areas, and I hate to make that statement in a way. Fire building is a ritual that mankind has always engaged in. It's a comforting ritual which used to keep the glowing eyes of sabertooth tigers beyond the rim of light, away from the mouth of the cave. We are all fire builders; it's a part of the intricate net that makes us human. However, we just can't afford to indulge our atavism in an overcrowded wilderness any longer.

In many areas, we have no choice. If you're backpacking in the White Mountains National Forest, you don't build fires, period, and most National forests either require a fire permit or flatly ban campfires. You can still build a campfire in the Adirondacks, but the rangers can ban all fires in dry seasons. Many states prohibit fire-building on private lands without the direct permission of the owner. In Maine, you can build a fire where the state tells you to. Be sure to check the fire regulations and conditions for the area you want to pack to.

There are times when a cooking fire is appropriate, or even necessary, so we should learn how to build one to do the job with essentially no impact on the surroundings. You don't need a huge blaze, either. Begin by finding a good place for the fire. Chances are, in the Northeast, that you'll have to prepare one. Begin by scraping away the loose, combustible forest duff in a small, rectangular area, maybe a foot wide by two feet long. Don't scatter the duff around; put it in a pile where you can get at it later. Down to something that looks like it won't torch off when you look at it? Dirt is fine. Now find some smallish, flat rocks and arrange them down the sides of the rectangle. While you're at it, find one rock that'll close off one end of the rectangle. This is your draft control. Leave it in place or move it as you need.

Now your fireplace is ready. All you need is wood. With a little rooting around, you can find a lot of dead and down branches and twigs. You don't need anything bigger around than your thumb for this exercise, really, and some smaller stuff will be very useful to get the larger pieces going.

There are two good ways to build a small cooking fire, and you can find them written up in massive detail in a lot of books, the best still being old Kephart's *Camping and Woodcraft.* The first is the teepee method, in which you arrange a pile of tinder and finely broken twigs in the center of a conical structure of larger twigs. An easier method is the grid, which isn't quite as fast, but isn't as fussy, either. The grid starts with a bundle of dry tinder, like the teepee, but it's formed by a crisscross arrangement of sticks. Start with a couple of good-sized sticks, laid parallel to the long side of your fireplace. Lay a row of small twigs across these, leaving a little space between them. Lay another row across these, and so on, with larger sticks on the upper layers. For cooking, let the fire burn down to coals, and rake most of them to the far end of the pit. This way, you can cook over a low, controlled heat source, and keep feeding your original fire so that it can provide more coals.

What happens if it's wet? Well, dead and down wood is pretty dry to begin with, and usually only the bark is wet, so the solution should be simple. Strip off the bark. If you need kindling, take your trusty knife and cut some twigs into small strips. That's right. Cut away from you, and if your knife gets dull, give it a lick and a promise on your pocket stone. If you're really desperate, a **small** dose of Boy Scout water from your handy fuel bottle — not over a couple of snootfuls from the eyedropper — will help immeasurably. Sure, it's cheating, but it works. Another gimmick that helps is a bit of aluminum foil under the tinder to reflect the heat. Contrary to popular opinion, this won't burn up, so when you're finished, stuff it in your garbage sack and **carry it out.**

When you've finished with the fire, drown it, stir it up, and drown it again, even if you're going to use this site the next morning. Fireproof your thinking, pal, and you won't have to fireproof your tent.

When you're ready to leave, and the fire is thoroughly drowned (get right in there with your pinkies and **feel** if it is), put the rocks back where they came from, sooty sides down, and rearrange the pile of duff over the pit. In a day or two, no sign will remain of your passing, and the next guy will find an "untouched" landscape. May he treat it as kindly as you did!

In fact, you can go a long way toward insuring that he will if you take some of that slack time you have before and after dinner to break down and restore that muzzy, random collection of fire areas. Pick up the trash, and pack out what you can't burn on the site, and make the place look good again. Sure, it's messy work, but this kind of gospel spreads quickly, and in time even the heavily-used areas will be a lot more pleasant.

This "clean fire" idea extends to a whole concept of camping that we're going to have to practice in today's crowded wilderness. Obviously, a clean cooking area's just a part of it. If you think about it for a bit, you'll recognize other ways to reduce the impact of your presence. Begin by not shortcutting trails. A switchback is there to provide a less steep grade so that water runoff doesn't erode the trail. If you shortcut the switchback, you set up an alternate runoff path, and water being the slave of gravity that it is, the steeper runoff path will be followed. The next thing you know, you have a fine, healthy gully that will wash out your trail. If you're into peakbagging, remember that the summits of most mountains in the Northeast are sub-Arctic terrain, and that the flora on them are slow-growing, shallow-rooted and terribly fragile. Don't tromp all over the summit. Stick to the existing paths and resist the temptation to bring back a souvenir flower.

Bushwhacking, that fine art of trailless travel, is a delight to the experienced woodsman, and there are a lot of lovely places that can be reached only by bushwhacking. Most of the time, there is an informal, unmarked "herd path" to these places. Sometimes it's easy to follow; other times it's tricky. Try to find that herd path if you can before you go stomping off in all directions, breaking branches down by the hundreds in an effort to blaze out a trail. The environment will little note your passing if you leave the vegetation intact, but every damn fool and his brother will recognize a lop blaze, and follow along.

Soon there's another herd path established going to the same place. No herd path is ever perfectly straightforward. People go off on random scoots, and come back again. People try a promising shortcut that winds up stymied in the pucker-bush. People take a wrong turn and slug out another variation on the path. It's bad enough without the added confusion of seventeen dim traces all headed the same way in seventeen highly idiosyncratic directions. So, bushwhacker, either follow the existing herd path or do your own thing without blazing your way. Save the forests — and save your less skillful followers from the delicious terror of an im-promptu bivouac in the boonies.

So much for zero-impact walking. Let's consider a few techniques for zero-impact camping as well. See that fine, sun-struck clearing over there? Could have been an old logging camp site, or maybe an old burn area. A good place to bunk in for the night, you say. Maybe a good place for a base camp for several days of hiking. But after two days, there will be an ugly rectangle of dead vegetation under your tent if you're at or above 2500 feet in the Northeast! All the world will know of your stay in that meadow for quite some time. Please don't just plop your tent down any old place! Look around a bit. Think of how your camp will alter the looks of the place after you've moved on. Camping in an Eastern clearing is a no-no. Camping in an Alpine meadow in the West is even more of a no-no, and is, in fact, prohibited in some of the National Parks. So truck off to the trees on the fringe of the clearing, friend. The meadow grasses will love you for it, and the mosquitos that dwell therein will not find you. The next hikers through will see no trace of your habitation.

Speaking of traces of habitation, you must realize that garbage is not to be tossed casually away, and that you don't just saunter off and crap on the ground behind your tent, leaving a toilet paper flower adorning the nearest shrub. Somehow, it's Un-American to think about garbage and about our own bodily wastes, but if we don't start soon, our more desirable areas are going to look (and smell) like feedlots. It isn't tough to be sanitary. The little microscopic beasties in the soil will do it for you if you let them. Just dig a shallow hole, not over a foot deep, and dump your garbage into that, or use that as your latrine. Leave your toilet paper in the hole, and torch it with a match. It'll help cut down odors. Then cover it. It's that sim-ple, and the rest of us don't have to share your leavings after you've gone. Needless to add, don't locate your latrine and your garbage hole right by the brook!

"Zero-impact camping!" Damn, that's a lofty phrase. Well, maybe it'll stick better in some heads than its more straightforward synonym, "good manners". Of course some people aren't ever going to learn; so when you clean up after them, reflect on this truism: Only trash make trash.

10. KEEPIN' THE WEATHER OUTSIDE

> *"If I'd never felt the sunshine, Lord,*
> *I would not curse the rain. . . ."*
> *— Billy Joe Shaver*

Time was when the Yankee backpacker could head for the outback with the assurance that somewhere around the trail's end a leanto would be waiting for him. An admirable invention, the leanto, born out of the great age of wilderness tripping in the Adirondacks of the nineteenth century. If you depend on finding a vacant one for shelter today, you're going to sleep wet and cold an awful lot of the time. There simply aren't enough leantos to go around, and there aren't going to be any more built. In fact, New York State's Master Plan for the Adirondacks recommends tearing down leantos in high-use areas. They're being phased out in the Whites, and those that the public hasn't destroyed through carelessness or lawlessness in the Greens are on the way out also.

The State of Maine has, in the past, liked the idea of well-defined camping areas, with or without leantos. Much of Maine's hiking and canoe camping territory lies within or close to private timberlands. Fire hazards are high, and a modicum of control is necessary.

So the handwriting's on the wall for all of us who enjoyed the leanto in the past. We're all going to be forced to carry our shelter with us, and it's about time. Sure, I'll miss the leanto. But I won't miss the overflowing garbage pit behind it, the moronic scribblings on the walls, the broken bottles, or the reeking outhouse that half of the time became an adjunct to the garbage pit.

The simplest form of shelter you can carry is a tarp, of 4-mil plastic or of coated nylon. The plastic tarp, usually called a "polytarp", is the least expensive shelter you can carry, although it's not terribly durable. Often you can buy a polytarp in a configuration called a tube tent, which is a step up in sophistication. If I have a beef against the polytarp or the tube tent, it's that they are so low-priced that a lot of people will leave a torn one in the woods rather than pack it out. I've counted *eight* polytarps abandoned around the Calamity Brook leanto complex in the Adirondacks. It's too easy to abandon a wet, torn tarp that only costs $1.50, but ditching a $20 coated nylon tarp because it's wet is something else.

Four-mil plastic is useful, but relatively fragile, and it grows brittle with age. It's easily mended in the field with a chunk of tape, and it's cheap. An 8' x 10' tarp is adequate for one person, and will do for two in simple configurations. A 10' x 12' (most poly comes in ten feet wide rolls) can provide cozy shelter for three or four people. Polytarps usually come in clear plastic, although some shops carry them in orange, which some prefer for privacy. I don't know why. If you're a privacy freak, stay away from tarps of any color, because they afford about as much privacy as a locker room shower.

The first articles to procure for yourself are some Visklamps at your friendly local outfitter's. A Visklamp is an ingenious little gadget that looks like an old-fashioned lady's garter. And it comes with a small rubber ball. Before it's lost, stuff it into a corner of the tarp, poke it and the material through the large hole in the clamp, slide the whole mess through into the small hole and pull tight. Presto. A garter for a polytarp that won't cut the poly. A pebble or a small pine cone will do in lieu of the ball, and the pebble held by a wrapping of parachute cord will work better than the whole arrangement.

But a Visklamp, like a safety pin, just does the job a bit better. This elegantly simple device was created originally to hold polytarp in place on farms, and to erect black polyshade frames for tobacco growing. I like to have enough of them along to provide for a clamp at regular intervals around the periphery of the tarp. An 8' x 10' for example, might be clamped like this:

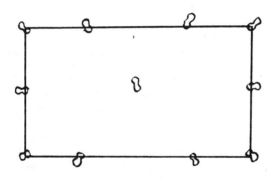

This seems like a lot of clamps. It is. Most of the time you won't need them. But in a wind-driven rain, you might want to do this:

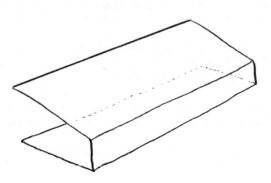

To hold this firmly, you need eleven clamps. You also need some propitiously placed shrubbery. In the Northeast that's hardly a problem. If you balk at using that much chute cord, by the way, try dental floss. It's strong, cheap, excellently packaged – and you can use it to clean your teeth, too! Just don't leave it dangling from the trees. Cut it all off, pocket it, and throw it away later or burn it.

Nylon tarps range from flimsy junk with tiny lengths of sleazy tape stitched on them at random spots to real neaty 1.9 or 2.2 ounce coated ripstop nylon ones with brass grommets set in reinforcements every two or three feet along the edges and cordura tie laces bar-tacked in the center. The difference in price is maybe five bucks. If you like tarps, or if you can't afford a good tent, get a **good** nylon tarp. Don't let anybody tell you that all nylon is the same, either. A tarp is probably bombproof if it looks and feels that way.

An alternative is the old Gerry Pioneer tent, a tarp with mosquito netting at both ends and a zipper down each side. You can zip it up and you have a one-man tent with a somewhat lumpy floor, or you can unzip it and have a two-man floorless shelter with mosquito net. A neat little beast, and it works tolerably well. Unfortunately, no tarp or tarp tent is truly the answer in the Northeast.

For that, you have to go to a tent. And tents, good ones, are expensive. Watch out for cheap ones. They'll louse up your precious, hard earned time in the boondocks. They don't pitch properly, they come apart at the seams, their poles break, and they leak. You're as well off with a tarp as with a poor tent. Better off, in fact. You've invested less money and not had any false expectations aroused. So expect to lay out some bucks for a decent tent if you're going the tent route.

The two commonest materials for tentage are cotton poplin and nylon. In this technological age, cotton tentage is still around. Its best is superb – quite watertight, admirable breathability, and it pitches well. However, cotton is heavy and must be dried meticulously. It gains weight appreciably when wet, and almost costs as much as a high-quality nylon tent. You'll go a bundle for good poplin tents for backpacking, and you'll only get them from three sources: Thomas Black & Co., Ogdensburg, N.Y., or dealers who carry Black's gear; Laacke & Joys in Milwaukee, who make their own and sell only through their catalog; or Eureka Tent and Awning in Binghamton, N.Y., makers of the estimable Blanchard Draw-Tite design. You won't get burned by a canvas tent from either Black's or Laacke & Joys, and Eureka does a good job on the Draw-Tite.

Nylon tents come in a bewildering array of types and fabrics. Cheapest is the single-layer coated nylon tent. In my considered opinion over many years of hiking, canoeing, and outfitting, these tents won't keep you dry when it rains. Let's review some of the failings of these billowing horrors.

Sailmakers seem to have been the designers. They fill with the slightest breeze and can't be drawn snug. This is a function of design as well as a function of fabric cutting. It's cheaper to cut straight panels and make your cuts parallel to the selvage. A function of assembly limits the ability of the fabric to stretch. They're sloppily assembled; seams wander drunkenly along, the fabric is savaged into place in great puckers, and nothing ever quite lines up. You can't square up the floor because you'll pull them out if you tug a bit. The pull-outs are given a perfunctory lick and a promise by a machine, but they're hardly ever backstitched, let alone bartacked, or

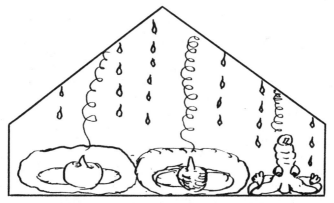

COATED NYLON TENTS DON'T BREATHE

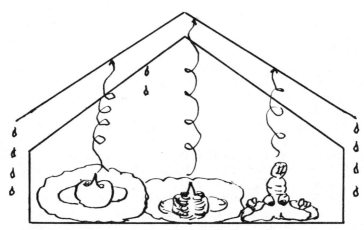

CONDENSATION'S MINIMIZED IN A
TENT WITH AN UNCOATED ROOF AND
A COATED RAINFLY SUSPENDED
ABOVE IT.

boxed, and the pull-out is never backed by another swatch of fabric. Pull too hard, and the thing rips out. And the poles? I'd rather build my own out of empty beer cans.

The chief horror is that the single-layer coated nylon tent doesn't work at all for the Easterner. Built impeccably, outfitted with affection, designed in a wind tunnel if you will. Use it in the Sierras for years. But not in the humid East of protracted rains. The single-layer tent simply condenses so much moisture inside that your gear gets wet. In truth, you're better off with a tarp, and far better off with a heavy, fussy, eminently biodegradable poplin tent than you are with a single layer of coated nylon.

The answer, at least at present, is a double-wall tent. The tent floor and sidewalls (up six inches to a foot) are sewn of coated nylon, and the tent body is of uncoated nylon. Uncoated nylon is not waterproof. Pitched very snugly, it is at best slightly water-repellent. Nylon absorbs next to no moisture, so it can't swell up like cotton and fill the weave to keep water droplets out but still permit air to pass through. So, over this relatively porous, breatheable membrane, you suspend a waterproof flysheet of coated nylon. Air circulating under the flysheet will dissipate the bulk of your foul miasmas (you exhale a pint of water vapor and halitosis every night). The rest will condense on the flysheet and glide tremblingly to the ground. Mostly. Sure, you'll condense a bit, but not much.

Okay. All your good tents are made this way, and a fair number of bad ones. How can you tell one from the other? Price. The good tent market is so bitterly competitive, and the backpacking shops so equipment oriented, that a bummer simply won't survive if it masquerades as quality gear. Not that the customers won't buy it. The equipment freak who does the shop's buying stacks it up against the really good tents he knows about, and simply refuses to stock it. Not only that, he tells his customers that it's lousy, and tells them why. Sooner or later, the manufacturer has to dump his stuff to a closeout house where it then gets sold at the proper price. Unfortunately, the inflated price tag leads a lot of good people to think that they're getting a real bargain when they're not.

How do we pick out a good, serviceable tent for three-season use? What do we look for, besides just something with a fly over it? First, let's look at ourselves. I'm over 6'2", and my wife is tall, too. But we're both lean and we sleep close together. We exist nicely in a narrow (4'2") tent. The 4'11"width of my Alp is an unaccustomed luxury in summer. If you're restless, or claustrophobic, or into the more athletic positions in the Kama Sutra, you may want a wider two-man. Or even a three-man. We don't hole up in a rain. If we did, we'd like a roomier tent. For canoeing, where we may hole up for a day to fish or ride out a storm, we take the big tent. But for packing, the skinny old Gerry yearround (old style — much smaller than the new one) is just fine. If you'd prefer to read on a rainy day — which means you'll get in a lot of reading in the Northeast — you'll want a roomier tent. Don't worry about the extra weight. Be comfortable. You're not going out there to suffer but to re-create yourself.

Once you've made a decision about the size of the tent you'd like, then you're in a position to consider subtleties of design and fabrication. The first subtleties to consider aren't very subtle. Look at the tent as it's pitched on the floor at your friendly local outfitter's shop. Does it pitch smartly? Do the panels pull up tautly, without bagging and sagging? Good. Is the floor square, or are the seams sewn in a lovely free-hand that meanders all over? Square and snug? Groovy. Is there adequate ventilation in the tent? Is the rear window panel really big, so that air can move through the tent on a hot night, or is there just one chintzy little ventilator that looks like a misbegotten stovepipe? A big window? Fine. Look at the fly-sheet. Does it float well off the tent body, or does it drape listlessly against the tent? How about enough lines attached to it to stay away even in a hard, wind-driven rain? Yes? Good. Big enough to overlap the sidewalls a bit, and overlap the front and rear panels as well? Do you think you could leave the panels (door and window) open in a rain with some assurance of remaining dry? I don't mean a super-hard torrent, just a light rain. In a real gully-washer, it's psychically comforting to button up. Could you leave the tent partially open in a light rain? Great.

Now, and only now, crawl in. If you hike with your lady friend, bring her in with you. Easy to get into? No crummy single pole planted right in the middle of the door? Fine. The single-pole jobbies are often reasonably priced, and some are very well made for the bucks, but they're horrors to get into and out of. The A-frame arrangement is easier — and much more stable.

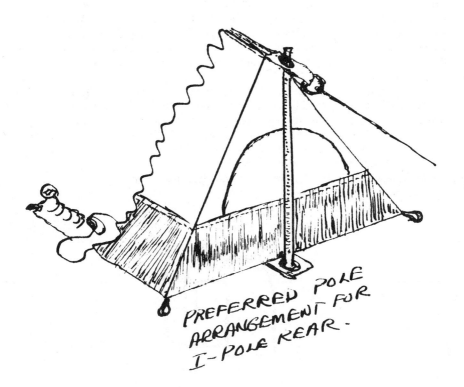

PREFERRED POLE ARRANGEMENT FOR I-POLE REAR.

You're not finished yet. This is your home away from home. Does it feel cozy to you? A good place to spend a rainy day on a canoe trip? Is the color appealing? Blue is fine but can be numbing on a dark day. My wife likes it. She says that it gives a secure, womblike feeling. I get antsy after a while, though. Orange is bright and cheerful, and great for skin tones, but the bright morning sun can be a bit over-powering. Color fine? Feel comfortable inside? Room enough for apartness as well as togetherness? Good. Now try the zippers on the screening, the storm flap, and the rear vent. Smooth? Easy to get at? Can you close the storm flap while you're ensconced in your sleeping bag, or do you have to be a gymnast to perform the feat? You can? You're all set.

Now that you're convinced that you can live in (and with) the tent, you can examine the construction details. If this procedure sounds backwards, there's a reason for it. A tent that you're comfortable in can be tinkered, assuming it's gen-erally well made, with the modest expenditure of some time and some thread. Don't coo over the latest supertent if you really don't like LIVING INSIDE the thing. Chances are that you don't need a supertent anyway. At any rate, ask your outfitter if you can take the tent down and re-erect it. This will give you the chance to see if it's too fussy for your tastes, as well as a good close look at the construc-tion details that really count.

Once the tent is down, roll it up and stuff it into its house. Does it fit? Just barely? It's a fine, tidy bundle there, in a warm dry shop, but on a cold, rainy day, will you have the patience to compress the tent that much? I don't. All my tents are in larger stuff sacks than they came in originally, and they're *easy* to fit in when they're wet. Usually you can con the outfitter into swapping the tent's stuff bag for a slightly bigger one. He's not going to blow a hundred dollar sale for two bits worth of nylon.

Now pitch the tent. Square up the floor, and while you're at it, check the stitch-ing where the floor is joined to the sidewalls and the sidewalls to the tent body. Two rows? And fairly fine stitching, eight to ten stitches to an inch? Look on the inside, too. Are the stitches as snug there as on the inside? If they're not, the seam was sewn with uneven tension on the bobbin and downfeed, and the thread can be cut by chafing against the fabric more readily.

Do the seams look like they've been joined like this?

It could be better, but it's acceptable if the edges have been hot-cut. Far better is this seam:

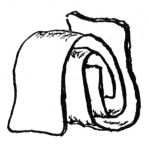

It's also more expensive, but everything's tucked in neatly, and there's nothing to unravel. If you run across something like this, walk away. It's junk.

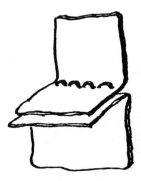

Take a look at the little loops you use to stake out the corners of the tent. Sturdy? Looks like miniature seat belts? Okay. Are they set into the seams and bar-tacked in place? Here's a bar tack:

It's actually a very, very tight zigzag stitch, and it really locks the loops in place. If there are grommets in the loops to accommodate the bottom end of the A-poles, do they look like they'll be around a year from now? I can't give you any rules about detecting shoddy grommets after they're installed except that intangible thing called "feel". A cheap grommet looks and feels *cheap*.

With the floor neatly skewered, assemble the front pole set. If it's an A-pole, the poles are usually strung together by shock cord or heavy elastic. If it's a Gerry, the elastic is provided for you, and you string the poles yourself. Do it, by the way. It eases confusion on a dark night, and keeps the poles warm and happy and TOGETHER. Do the poles look and feel solid, or do they look like the first light breeze will buckle them? Do they fit in the pockets well? Do the pockets look like they'll stand the gaff of wind loading, or are they sewn on in dime-store fashion? Erect the front of the tent, but don't be overenthusiastic about it. Now to the rear. If a double A-frame is your bag, and they are lovely if you can bear the weight and the extra dollars, go through the same checkout.

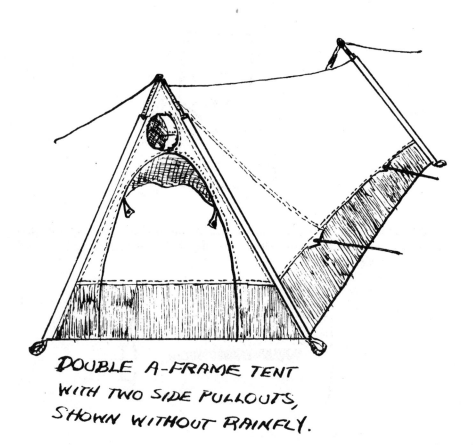

DOUBLE A-FRAME TENT WITH TWO SIDE PULLOUTS, SHOWN WITHOUT RAINFLY.

SAME TENT RIGGED
WITH RAINFLY FOR
THE SUNNY NORTHEAST

After you pitch your tent, look at it again. Straight and snug? Fine. No great hassle to pitch? Fine again. Check the front door. Zippers sewn in with several rows of stitching? Are the screen zippers sewn onto tape, or just onto a doubled-over netting? Onto tape? Good. The other will pull out with hard use. But if everything else is acceptable, it's easy enough to beef up the zipper attachment.

Now pitch the fly. Well-grommeted? Good. A sturdily attached nylon lace is also acceptable, but a grommeted fly is preferable. If the grommets are reinforced with a tab of leather or of heavy nylon, so much the better.

You'll notice I haven't said anything about material, and for a couple of good reasons. First, any tent that's well enough sewn to pass the above inspection is probably made of pretty good material. Second, you can't tell by inspection whether the material is good or just fair. Second-rate material is easy to tell, of course, but fine differentiations require a lot of experience in examining fabrics. Third, it's been my experience that a good tent can be made out of ripstop or out of taffeta. It simply doesn't matter. My old Alp is ripstop, and my little Gerry is taffeta. Both have proven to be bombproof in high wind and heavy snow because they're both well designed and well assembled. The fabric, be it ripstop or taffeta, is first-quality. In general, you can trust your instincts with fabric. If it feels good and looks good, it most likely is.

Up until now, I've been discussing a rather conventional two-man tent. I haven't gotten involved in the self-standing two mans, or the three or four man varieties, because designers have really gone hog wild on some of these creatures. There are dome tents; tents that look like butterflies; like great soaring flowers; like truncated tipis; and like big two-man tents too. Regardless of the design, an examination of the construction can be carried out "by the book". As for the design, it either makes it for you or it doesn't.

> As this book is being written, there's a furor breaking around my head about fireproof, or at least flame-retardant tents. I suppose that by the time this opus hits the street, a benign Federal Government will protect us all, at the cost of heavier, more costly, less durable and stiffer fabric for tentage. You shouldn't cook or use an open flame in your tent, nevertheless.

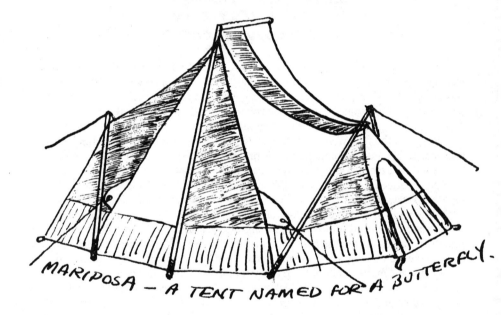

MARIPOSA — A TENT NAMED FOR A BUTTERFLY.

11. KNOWIN' WHERE YOU ARE

> *"I know where I am. I'm in the*
> *Adirondacks!"*
> *— Molly Stark Roberts*

As I write this, I'm looking at two maps on my office wall, the USGS topographical maps for West Canada Lakes and Indian Lake in New York's southern Adirondacks. It's an area that's been timbered over and trapped over for 150 years, and the land ownership pattern is a crazy quilt of public domain and private holdings. The maps are laced with dead-end trails into old logging camps, old military roads, and those little topographic features that indicate to the Adirondack rover that a settlement existed in a certain spot long before anybody cared about mapping this wilderness. On the map or not, most of these traces and byways have vanished. Nature, in the end, triumphed over these bold, hard men with double-bitted axes, and all that's left of their riotous passage is a set of dotted lines on a map, a slight difference in flora along a forgotten tote road, and the remains of a hundred-year-old logging camp gradually sinking into the forest duff.

You can recreate French Louie's trapline, bushwhack into a clearing called Sled Harbor, an old marshalling area for log sleds and trapper's sleds, roam the fringes of Camp 22, and cruise the Gould Tract, seeking out a vanished way of life. All you need is the ability to use a map and follow a compass, and the imagination to see a departed world beneath the impersonal contours of a top sheet. In other words, your ability to use a map and a compass gives you the freedom of the forests.

The requisite skills for woods wandering aren't difficult to attain. Let's go down to your friendly local outfitter and buy two things, a map and a compass. The map's easy. Ask for the U.S. Geological Survey map for the area you live in, or for a near-by area if you're a city dweller. While you're getting the map, look at the index sheet that your outfitter probably has on display. There's your state, broken up in lots of little rectangles. They're not all the same size. If you're an Easterner, the boxes come in two sizes. The larger one is the so-called 15 minute sheet, because it covers fifteen minutes of longitude. The smaller ones, four of which are necessary to cover a 15 minute sheet, are 7½ minute sheets. U.S.G.S. has embarked on a program to put the whole country on 7.5 minute sheets, but you gotta be patient. The 7.5 sheets have some definite advantages, as you can see. They're much easier to read. However, they cover such a small area that it's at times difficult to gain a broad view of the terrain. The 15-minute map is plotted on a scale of 1:62500, which means that one unit of measure on the map equals 62,500 units on the ground. This is close to the simple, easily remembered scale of one inch equals one mile. The 7½ minute sheet is plotted on a 1:24000 scale, or more simply, an inch equals 2,000 feet on the ground. Got your map? Fine. Now let's get a compass to go with the map.

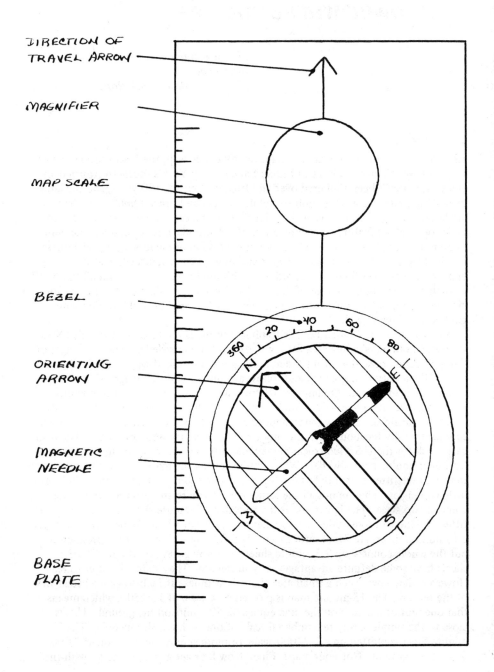

DIRECTION OF TRAVEL ARROW

MAGNIFIER

MAP SCALE

BEZEL

ORIENTING ARROW

MAGNETIC NEEDLE

BASE PLATE

THE PARTS OF A COMPASS

You want a compass that's mounted on a transparent plastic plate to facilitate map work. You also want a liquid-filled compass, because the needle comes to rest much more quickly with this type than with the less expensive induction-damped unit, and it stays put so you can read it more accurately.

In the lower left hand margin of the map in front of you, there's technical information on how the mapping was done and to what bases. To the right of that is a little collection of lines and arcs that looks like a problem in geometry. It tells you that true north (straight up on the map) and magnetic north aren't the same in most places in North America, which means that your compass and your map aren't exactly in line unless you live along a wavy line that passes through such eminent wilderness areas as Grand Rapids, Michigan, and Knoxville, Tennesse. The difference between your compass and your map is expressed in that angle called *declination.* You can adjust for this angle of declination with ease, without buying an expensive compass. The time will come when map and compass work sneaks up on you and you become a map freak, but that takes time. All you want for the present is that simple board-mounted, liquid-filled compass.

What your outfitter will probably hand you is a Silva Polaris, or possibly a slightly larger (and slightly more expensive) Silva model, although you may see a Suunto. You can't do any better for the price than any of these, and you can do a lot worse. Take a minute and check out your purchase. There isn't a bubble in the case, is there? Good. Does the needle swing freely? Fine. Now check your instrument against a handful of others in the dealer's supply. Don't set them side by side — they won't like that a bit. All of them point toward the bow of the Moore Venom competition cruising canoe on the wall? Good. Close enough. The compass works. Okay! No bubbles, no impairment in needle motion, general agreement as to the location of magnetic north. You got yourself a compass.

The first step in using a compass is the acceptance of an article of faith. The compass is always right. There may be a time when it isn't. You could, for example, be standing over a heavy concentration of iron ore — although more probably your steel belt buckle. The first is rare, and the second correctable.

You're a believer? Good. Now let's look at what you can do with a compass and map. The first doesn't require a map at all, actually. It's called walking a field bearing. The situation may read like this. You're on top of a little hill. There's a pond in the distance. It's not too far, but far enough that you won't be able to see it when you drop down off the rise. It's not on the map, either. There's a stream shown, but no pond. Point the direction arrow on the compass base plate toward the pond, and turn the dial (called a bezel in formal parlance) until the red end of the magnetic needle points toward 360 degrees. The direction arrow's tail intersects the compass bezel at a certain number of degrees. That's your bearing. Keep the magnetic needle over the orienting arrow on the bottom of the rotating bezel. It's an easy, accurate check on your heading.

Start walking toward the pond. As long as the pond's in sight, there's no problem, but as you drop off the ridge and into the puckerbush, you must rely on that skinny little arrow. Stop. Reorient your compass to the correct bearing just to be sure, and pick out a distinct landmark ahead that lies on your path of travel, such as a big tree or rock. Go to it, reorient again, pick another landmark, and keep on trucking. Sooner or later, you'll hit the pond.

There's also a simpler way. If that pond's a little five acre job two miles away, you could conceivably miss it if you tried to hit it accurately in the middle. You know there's a stream flowing out of it, though. Take a conservative bearing downstream. Simple. You could manage this without a compass if you had to, but hitting the pond in the middle without a compass would be pure dumb luck. If you want to retrace your steps to the top of the rise from the pond, you follow a back bearing. It's simple. Let's say that the course you walked on the way out was 78 degrees. Add half a circle to that figure, or 180 degrees, giving you a bearing of 258 degrees to follow. If your original bearing was more than 180, subtract 180 from it. If you walked out on a bearing of 210 degrees, subtract half a circle and you have a thirty-degree bearing to walk back. Use the same tree-sight technique and you'll be back on the ridge in no time.

This is fine — unless you find a healthy swamp barring your way between the ridge and the pond. You could slog on through it, but there's an easier way. You know from observation and from the contour lines on the map that the valley you're traversing tilts downhill, as it were, to your left. Try the high side of the swamp for easier passage. You're walking a bearing of 78 degrees already, so you'll make a 90-degree turn to your right. Your bearing is now 78 plus 90, or 168 degrees. Sight against some prominent landmark and start walking. But this time, count every double step you take, and jot the number down in your little notebook. Go far enough to clear the obstacle. Turn left 90 degrees, which puts you back on your original bearing, and walk that until you're sure you're across the swamp. Then turn left. For this, you'll subtract 90 degrees from your original bearing of 78 degrees, and you'll walk a bearing of 348 degrees. Zero and 360 are coincident, aren't they? No problem. Think of it as minus twelve, if you wish — as long as the direction of travel arrow and 348 degrees are lined up, and the magnetic needle is oriented with the orienting arrow.

Here's the tricky part. When you first turned right off your original course, you walked 350 double steps. When you turned left, to "cross" the swamp, how far you traveled didn't matter. But this left turn will take you back to the original line you were following — and the best way to get there, short of carrying a surveyor's chain, is to walk that same 350 double steps along that 348 degree heading. When you've done that, turn right again, reorient your compass, take a field bearing of 78 degrees and march boldly on, smiling the smug smirk of the newly informed.

Working from a map is totally different. You don't have to worry about declination, that difference between true north and magnetic north, when you're following a field bearing, but you do when you're working from a map. If the declination is small, say one degree or thereabouts, you can forget about it unless you're a true map and compass freak, but the 14-degree declination you face in the Adirondacks is considerable. In fact, it can mean about a quarter-mile error for each mile of travel, which is an imposing chunk of territory. There are two ways to handle declination. The first, and most commonly used, is as follows:

Place the compass on the map so that the long edge of the compass board connects the two points between which you want to travel. Next, rotate the bezel of the compass until the orienting arrow (NOT the needle — the orienting arrow) is pointing true north. On USGS sheets, this is parallel to the side of the map. Your bearing will be where the direction of travel arrow intersects the compass housing. Note that figure, though. If you were walking a simple field bearing, that would be it. But to compensate for declination, you have to add or subtract the degrees of declination from your bearing. In the Adirondacks, that's roughly 14 degrees west. In fact, until you get into Florida, central and western Tennessee, and western Kentucky, your eastern maps will always show a west declination. If the declination is west, add it to your field bearing. If it's east, subtract it. There's an old rhyme that will help you remember that — East is least, and West is best.

I've always thought of that as the hard way to do it. I correct my maps before I use them. Here's how. Remember the declination arrow? Take a straightedge and extend that line all the way across the map with a pencil or a ball point. Then use your straightedge to draw parallel lines to it covering the map.

With these lines drawn, life is simpler. Connect the two points you wish to travel between with your compass base plate, swing the bezel until the orienting arrow is parallel with one of the magnetic north lines you've drawn, and read your bearing where the direction of travel arrow intersects the bezel. This way you don't have to correct for declination.

I'd like to think that it was all this simple, but it never turns out to be. Here's a common example. You've parked your car along an unfamiliar dirt road that runs sort of east-west to scramble through some hackberry to an attractive little hill about a mile and a half off the road. There isn't a trail, and you don't have a map, but your faithful Polaris is sitting in your daybag. Great. You can see the hill from the road, and your field bearing is exactly due north. Off you go, following the landmark to landmark procedure we've talked about. In a bit less than two hours, you're on top of the hill, and the view is certainly pretty. It was worth the sweat.

Later, you head on back to the car. It's a simple enough back bearing. Due south. In due time you arrive at the road. Hmmm. No car. Oh, well, should be just up the road a piece. Dunno. This doesn't look familiar. Maybe it's down the road a piece. Damn. Which way is it? Off you go, up the road. After a half mile or more, you're convinced it isn't that way, so you turn around. It starts to rain. You burrow into your daybag for your poncho and, ohmigod, that's right, the kids took it to camp. Ouch. Back down the road at a fast trot as the skies open up. Around the corner from where you came out of the woods is your car. You climb in, drenched and muttering imprecations. "Damn compass is wrong. Damn that Roberts guy. He didn't tell me the right things to do! Mumble. Grizzle, grouse, grouse, DAMN!" To top it off, your matches are wet and you don't even have the solace of a pipeful of tobacco.

Well, you've been had by the commonest mistake of the novice map and compass freak. Take this as solace. The error here is easy to spot. Unless you're incredibly meticulous, and use a very accurate sighting compass like a Brunton, you're not going to be able to run a bearing much closer than one degree. This isn't much of an error, but it's enough to confuse you with roads and streams. The solution is equally evident. Instead of running a due south back bearing, run a bearing of maybe 185 degrees. No, you won't arrive at your car, but you're certain that you'll arrive on the road somewhere a bit to the west of your car. Then it's simple. Turn left at the road, and you'll find your car.

This is all well and good. You know how to follow a compass bearing, how to develop one from a map and follow it, and how to establish a base line, which is the fancy name for finding your way back to the car parked along the road. What happens if you've been wandering about without following your compass and you'd like to know where you are? If you have a map, the compass will help. If you don't it will help you get out of trouble, but it can't tell you where you are. First the map.

You've dropped off the trail and headed up the side of a knob that you thought was a satellite peak to a mountain you wanted to climb, but you've been charging along now for some time, and you have that distinctly uneasy feeling that you're not where you think you are. No trouble, but inconvenient and embarrassing. You know where you are well enough to beat back down the hill and pick up the trail that runs along its foot, but that's a long way. Off in the distance, you spot two prominent peaks and a lot of smaller ones. You recognize one of them, and it's fairly easy to determine what the other one is from the map. You now have two known points to work from, and you have your map out and oriented. Take a back bearing of one peak. Sight **against** the direction of travel arrow on your compass and turn the housing until the north part of the needle is in line with the orienting arrow. Now you have the magnetic back bearing, which you read off the bezel where the direction of travel arrow intersects it. Now put the compass on the map, with one back corner touching the peak. Swing the base plate, using the peak as the axis of rotation, until the orienting arrow is parallel to a magnetic north-south line. Draw a line along the edge of the compass. You're somewhere along this line. In some situations, that one point would be enough for you to have a fair idea of your location, especially if the landmarks of the area are prominent. If you're really confused, though, you need to take the backbearing of the other peak you recognized in the distance, and do the same thing. After you've drawn your second line, you'll note that the lines cross. You are sitting where the lines cross.

The first clear day you get, take your map and compass out in the field and practice with them. Learn to orient the compass and the map, learn to follow field bearings and back bearings, practice walking from and returning to a base line, and try your hand at resection in known territory. Take this book along, if you think you'll need it. Take a friend along, too. It may help if the friend knows compass work, but if he doesn't you can both learn together. And take a relaxed, easy head.

One afternoon fiddling with a compass in a more or less organized way will tell you everything you'll ever need to find your way. If your chosen area has a hill with a good view, you'll find out a lot about those lines and symbols on the map as well. Most of them are evident. The broken line symbol indicates a trail. This doesn't mean that the trail's still there, of course. If the date of the map in the lower right hand corner is fairly recent, it may be. If it's an oldie, don't depend on it. Don't depend on finding all the unimproved roads indicated by a double row of broken lines, either, although a little judicious woodcraft and poking around will enable you to find a log road that's been unused for fifty years and covered with underbrush.

The only markings on a top sheet that might not be self-explanatory are those miserable wiggly brown lines running all over the place. They're called *contour lines,* because they form a picture of what the contours of the terrain look like. The theory is simple. A contour line is an imaginary line on the ground along which the elevation above sea level is constant. Sometimes another base is used, but don't sweat it. The difference in elevation between contour lines is called *contour interval,* and it appears on the bottom margin of the map, in the center, right under the scales. It's typically twenty feet on the 15 minute maps and ten feet on the 7½ minute maps. The heavy lines indicate 100 foot intervals, while the thin lines are as stated on the map. If you follow one of the heavy lines long enough, you'll probably find a number on it, usually in brown print. This is the elevation, and the brown print tells you that it is calculated from aerial photographs by photogrammetric methods. Figures in black have been verified in the field. If you look at the contour lines of a familiar ridge while you're looking at the ridge itself, you'll soon see how they work. So much for the difficulties of map and compass work.

Most of the old woodsman's lore about finding your way breaks down on close examination. Moss, regrettably, grows on all sides of a tree. But a little observation and one trick can save the day even if you should lose your map and break your compass. The trick is simple. If you point the hour hand of your watch toward the sun, due south is halfway between the hour hand and twelve. Obviously, if your watch is set on Daylight Saving Time, the trick isn't as accurate. Without a watch you could take an educated guess as to the time and ballpark a southerly direction.

Another trick is simply looking around. If you're worried about getting there, or trucking along so fast that you're seeing nothing but your bootsoles, you're not at all receptive to the passing terrain. If you'd been aware, or stopped for a breather and a look at the lay of the land, or poked around smelling the wildflowers, you'd have heard a stream running off the trail. It was never close enough to see, but you'd followed it in all the way. If you could find that stream, you could pick up the trail again. But you can only know the stream's there if your mind's free and loose and receptive to the rustle of moving water. There's a fire watch tower on that little peak at the end of the range down there. If you'd stopped along the trail and looked around, you would have seen it before, and you'd know that you'd been walking away from it all morning. A quartered look over your shoulder would have told you. Just simply stopping, turning around, and looking back down the trail (or down your bushwhack route) every now and then can give you a lot of information. Observe. That's the best insurance against getting lost. That and a map and a compass and your wits.

But what if you get lost? Nothing. You have food, probably, although you don't need it. It takes weeks to starve. Water is generally easy to find, and you have a canteen. You have extra clothing and raingear. Except for suddenly harsh weather, you're in no danger at all, believe me, unless you make the danger for yourself by lapsing into a bad case of the screaming jeaslies and running yourself into a sweating, exhausted blob of jelly.

If you can't spot a familiar landmark, you should at least have some idea of what general direction you followed walking out. You also have an idea of whether you've been gaining elevation or losing it. If there has been any sun at all, even a dull glow, you most likely have a good idea of where it was. In your face? Over your right shoulder? At your back? All right. You have, when you think about it, a lot of information and enough clothes to keep you warm and dry, a couple of bars of Hershey's Tropical Chocolate squirreled away in your pack, and some good daylight left. You're in good shape, if you think about it for a minute. I'll bet that with a little patience, you might even be able to locate some signs of your passage, at least for the last couple hundred yards or so. I'd also bet that you could drop down off that brushy knoll you're on into the valley and find a trail, if this is hiking country.

You may not know where the trail leads, but it has to go somewhere. If you're really confused, keep your movements lateral. Don't go in any deeper. Drop down the hill, or up the hill to catch a view, but don't contour the ridge purposelessly. If you're still clueless, park yourself, nibble a piece of chocolate, relax, and enjoy it. If you're not home tonight, there will be searchers out in the morning, for sure. Stay put and let them find you. If you're on a backpacking trip, you have enough gear to insure not only that you'll survive but that you'll flourish. Stay put and wait, and reflect on that sage advice about adversity — if it's inevitable, relax and enjoy it.

Write a poem to somebody you love, listen to the wind working easy in the treetops, run your hands through the rich forest duff, feel the bark of the pine tree against your back, and think about the next trip you'll take. There's a place out back of beyond, around the headwaters of Little Squaw Brook, in the deep valley between Buck Mountain and Snowy Mountain. Bet there was a logging camp in there in the old days. Be an easy skid down to Cedar River Flow. Maybe there — maybe down further between Onion Hill and Lewey Mountain. Now there's a damn fine bushwhack. None of that herd path nonsense. Take the canoe down the flow as far as it'll go, then strike off into the timber.

See you there. Just remember your maps and compass, because I'll probably forget mine.

12. GETTIN' THERE – TOGETHER

*"Where to now? Back through the
Enchanted Forest?"*
— *Teresa Dick*

Look at that map reclining supinely in front of you. Hardly any distance at all
between Blackfly Flow and Fuel Cartridge Clearing is there? The guidebook to the
Hookworm Range tells you that it's a mere 8.27 miles. Another glance at the map
shows a couple of ridges to cross on the way, and the guidebook notes one of them
as moderately steep. Since somebody's concept of fairly steep can differ drastically
from yours, it might be useful to translate some Guidebookeese into Beginning
Backpacker for you.

People who are afficionados of any active sport tend to forget the fact that they
did a lot of suffering when they began. A trip that I'd call a good little walk today
would destroy me if I had just gotten up from a desk to try it with no prior experience. My most vivid recollection of this is not connected with hiking, but with
whitewater paddling, when I took my wife, a strong canoeist but with very limited
whitewater experience, down a particularly sporty stretch of the Upper Hudson in
the bow of my ancient slalom canoe, and scared the bejeezus out of her. I'm
perched on my little stern pedestal getting my jollies from the big bad standing
waves we're boring through, and laughing my helmet off whenever we'd spin into a
sousehole and the old scow would settle into the foam up to our armpits before
it'd rise to the river again. Fun! Whoopee! And it took me five years to get her
back onto moving water after that trip. I've seen countless hikers, usually men,
come into my shop and lament that their wives, girlfriends, kids, or office buddies
didn't seem interested in hiking after one trip with them.

Now, I'm not talking about the occasional jerk who has to prove how hard he is
by running everybody into the ground. I'm talking about normal, pleasant people
who simply forget that ten miles up and down over a trail is significantly different
than ten miles on level ground, and that adding the burden of a pack, even a light
one, increases the burden on the neophyte to the breaking point. Far better you
begin with a short trip, and find yourself hollering for more, than you bite off
more than your companions (and you) can chew. So let's look at that guidebook
again and do some translating.

Easy Terrain – This may be described in many ways. If the trail goes up a valley,
it's probably pretty easy. Lots of feeder trails into the peaks are easy, and your
guides usually define this type of trail walk as "easy", "moderate", "gently rolling",
or the like. You can assume that you can truck on along this kind of trail at a comfortable two miles an hour. Sure, you can walk faster, but this gives you lots of
looking time – and that's what you're there for.

Moderate Terrain – Some people like to use "moderate" as a synonym for "easy", on the assumption that no trail is easy for a beginner. It's the kind of trail that may have one long hill, but not the steep, "stair-step" type, or it may have a lot of little, steep, thirty-foot bumps on it. You can still make your two miles an hour on it, but it won't be quite as easy, and you'll have less time for gawking. Plan one and a half miles per hour and you'll have plenty of looking time.

Steep Terrain – Guidebooks are inevitably written by hikers, and when a hiker says "steep", or "from this point the trail ascends to . . ." or "the trail is all upwards to . . .", he means that it's tough sweaty walking for a novice. Most trails up Eastern mountains of any size average about 1000 feet elevation gain per mile of trail. This isn't a constant rise, either. Sometimes the trail is vaguely going up, and other times it's like climbing a ladder. An Eastern trail that's switchbacked has been laid out that way strictly for erosion control. Generally, the Eastern mountains are ascended in a very direct fashion, because it's tough to cut switchbacks in heavily forested country. Don't expect to charge up these slopes at much more than one mile per hour. If you're carrying a full pack in this kind of terrain, you'll find that a mile an hour is very realistic.

On level terrain, plan to average two miles an hour. On moderate terrain, plan for one and a half miles per hour, and on steep terrain, plan for one measly mile per hour. In simpler terms, plan for two miles an hour and knock off a half mile per hour for each five hundred feet you go up – *or down.* Down? Why down? Don't you go down a hill faster than you go up a hill? Yep. Especially when you come tumbling down it ass over elbow! Sure a lot of experienced hikers sort of "ski" down steep, rough terrain, but the key to that is the word "experience". As far as you're concerned, a mile per hour up is a mile per hour down, until you know otherwise. Also, if there's a choice view on the way, or a mountaintop, add another hour to your overall walking time. After all, you're there to soak in the countryside, not to run a cross-country foot race.

Sure this is conservative, even with a full pack on your back, but I can't help repeating the simple idea that nobody enjoys his first trip when he's absolutely blown out by fatigue. So learn how to read that guidebook. Also learn how to translate what your experienced backpacking buddy tells you about a pet trip of his.

Speaking of first trips, sooner or later you'll wind up taking a friend or another member of your family with you. Let's assume you, Gentle Reader, are a guy. Normally healthy, been backpacking a few times, and interested in spreading the gospel. So, you decide that your neighbor (buddy, office mate, or the like) might enjoy this outdoorsy bit, and he sounds receptive. Your local outfitter rents some gear, so equipment isn't a hassle, and he's got a pair of well broken in hunting boots that aren't ideal but are at least comfortable. He's not a sit-in-front-of-the-tube sort of guy, but he's not as active as he should be, and certainly not consistently active. *This guy is a prime candidate for self-destruction,* and only you can prevent it. You can't baby another male. You can't take the larger chunk of the load like you could with a gal because you're simply considerably bigger and better engineered for carrying loads. And you can't do a super-short trip like you can with a kid.

The male animal, for better or worse, is a prideful beast, and likes to feel that he can do what any other man can do, by damn — and maybe a bit more. So give him his half of the load, plan a moderate trip that'll make your forehead break out with sweat a few times, and take your time doing it. Let your slightly out-of-shape buddy work hard enough to realize that he's been a trifle inactive lately, but don't run him into the ground just to prove how hard-assed you are. A fine line to walk, but if you value this dude's friendship, and you'd like to hike with him, don't set up some sort of pernicious little contest. I've seen enough of that puerile nonsense to patch hell a mile, and I've seen it blight a developing interest in a lot of people. Some of those who survived it turn out to be the biggest bunch of neo-sadists in the boondocks, gleefully running family and friends into the ground because they're still getting even. So take it easy. Not too easy, but easy. Just keep thinking that if you're hurting, and you're in shape, your buddy must be dying because he isn't. Slow down and the trip will go well.

By the way, some good, face-saving ways of giving a friend some much-needed respite on the trail are: 1) the bootlacing game, usable at least ten times in a six-mile trip; 2) the adjust-the-packstrap game, which can also be used to check out your pal's gear; 3) the conference-at-the-trail junction game, which can provide a good rest under the legitimate aegis of discussing an alternate route; 4) the camera game, which can be overdone to hell and gone if you're really into photography; and 5) the I'm-bushed, let's-take-a-break game, which is particularly useful on a long, long uphill slog. When you get to your destination, *you* do supper. After all, you know how to use the stove, and you know how to brew up whatever it is you're eating. Let your buddy stir the pot and relax.

Girls? Sure, occasionally you will find the Princess from Pelham Manor who's allergic to dirt, sweat, insects and baggy pants, but this is a symptom of a certain upbringing some people impose on women. Most girls aren't like that. But they're still smaller than guys, have less load-carrying capacity, and sleep colder than guys. Conversely, they're not hung up on a military bearing and gait, so they walk more easily and loosely than most guys. A gal's center of gravity is far more suited to good balance on rocky, miserable terrain. It isn't tough to figure out how to plan for a backpacking trip with a chick.

First, last and always — keep in mind that a woman's shoulders aren't generally as heavily muscled as a man's. They're hinged differently. A heavy load, some of which is supported by the shoulders in the best of packframes, will tear up a girl more quickly than a guy because it collapses her shoulder structure a bit more and actually robs her of a fair degree of her lung capacity. So, the first rule is that a woman shouldn't carry as much as a man of approximately equal weight. Sure, I know that there are exceptions. My wife is 5'10", 142 pounds, and a flatwater canoe racer to boot, which means all kinds of shoulder development. She's comfortable with about two thirds or less of what I'm comfortable with, and I'm a 152-pound 6'3" stringbean. The key word is, of course, "comfortable". We're not there to prove that we can outlift a packhorse. We enjoy ourselves, and that means being comfortable with our burdens. She carries less. Period.

That's really the key to it all. Give a girl a pack of a weight she can cope with, and she can walk your tail off, pal! As far as her sleeping colder than a guy, this shouldn't be a major hassle except in winter, which we're not discussing here. There are a couple of points, though, that you should keep in mind. Even in an age of long hair for men and women, most women still have longer hair than most men. A lot of your body's heat transfer takes place in the scalp and the nape of the neck. On a blazing hot day, the long-haired chick has more of a problem keeping cool. The hair has to go somewhere — either hanging over the nape of her neck or piled on her head. Pigtails? Pony tail? My wife tells me that either will work. It'll probably occur to her anyway, but a word or two in advance may not be amiss.

A word seems in order here on insects and insect repellent. Just my observation from a lot of backpacking points out that mosquitoes and black flies do attack women and kids more greedily than others. Check the insect repellent supply. And while you're there checking out your insect repellent, check your toilet paper supply. The Army tells us that bumwad consumption in the WACs is about 3½ times that of the guys. So, if you're backpacking with a chick, go heavy on the bumwad ration.

Kids are a whole 'nother smoke. They're not, as our Victorian forebears would have it, small adults. Neither are they little pure spirits trucking around in some luminous void like so many innocent butterflies. They're . . . well, they're *kids*. You were one once. And you'll remember, no doubt, that you had very little concept of goals as a kid. Kids live fiercely, and all their living is in the present. A promised view from a mountain top five miles away is five million miles away for them, but the poplar tree with the strange bump on its side is right now, and right now is to be looked at and questioned. Five miles from now will happen, maybe, but it's still in the future, and beyond thinking about. Come to think of it, it may behoove us all to let our head slide into a kid's view of the world more often. How many times have we charged on past something magical to get to the summit in time to take pictures? They're busy seeing as they go along; they're not worrying about getting to some distant summit. So if you're backpacking with kids, keep a very flexible schedule and ride with it.

On the more pragmatic side, kids can go like hell, but not for a long time. Be prepared to stop regularly. This, of course, is above and beyond those stops prompted by curiosity. It should also be evident that kids aren't very big, and shouldn't carry much. A hint here. Kids do like to please, and they like to participate. I'm of a mind that believes they need to participate. Accordingly, they should carry something, if only a tiny pack with a change of socks and a bowl and spoon in it. My preference for my little dudes is the Kelty sleeping bag carrier, which is sort of the top part of a teardrop-shaped daybag with a pair of straps sewn onto it for carrying a sleeping bag. The little pack will hold a sweater, a poncho, and a bowl and spoon. A kid's sized sleeping bag and foam pad fits underneath nicely. The lad carries at the most seven pounds, and really does his share of the work. Older kids, of course, can carry more, but you can also get an acceptable frame pack for the nine-year and up set. Jan Sport has a particularly full line for young backpackers. Frame pack or no, don't overload the little folk. Adults can carry a third of their body weight, and should carry about a fifth of it. For a kid, I'd have to call a fifth an absolute maximum, because weight really tears them apart.

In a sense, there's little difference between planning trips for any newcomer to the game, be that person a neighbor, a wife or girlfriend, or a youngster. All I've said in the palaver above can be boiled down to a single sentence: plan a trip that's within the capabilities of the people doing the trip. And don't forget to include yourself in that.

13. THE BLACK AND BLUE BACKPACKER

*"If it wasn't for bad luck, I wouldn't
have no luck at all."*
— Booker T.

There are so many sources of detailed first aid instructional material that to do a full-dress chapter on the topic would be like reinventing the wheel. I'm not going to talk about spectacular setbacks like broken bones, basal fractures of the skull, peritonitis, insulin shock, or even snakebite — except to comment that if you hike in snake country, you had better carry a snakebite kit and possibly even polyvalent antivenin. Severe injury in the field is best treated by somebody who really knows how to cope with the problem — and no book can teach that.

Fortunately, serious injury is rare. But a seemingly endless succession of little problems can ruin a pleasant trip. Let's look at some hints about coping with the little nuisances — and some major dangers as well that are amenable to treatment in the field.

INSECT BITES

The commonest unpleasant encounter is with the mosquito, followed closely by black flies, deerflies, gnats and noseeums. A healthy infestation of insects of the sort that could be measured in pounds per cubic foot is at best an annoyance and at worst a horror. The obvious solution is insect repellent. There are dozens on the market; some of them work much better than others. It's no coincidence that the effective ones contain a chemical called N, N-diethyl-metatoluamide, a true mouthful, commonly abbreviated "deet" even in the stately prose of the Army Quartermaster Corps. There are a few isomers of this long-chain molecule that have some repellent value, too, and you'll occasionally find them in repellents. Look for names like dimethyl phthalate, ethyl hexanediol and butopyronoxyl. Deet works better.

There is more to consider when buying a repellent, beside the fact that it contains deet. An alcohol base lotion or liquid evaporates quickly. While it may offer good protection, it doesn't last as long as a cream base or a synthetic wax base. I've had excellent results with Cutter's, which contains about 29 percent deet, and from a locally produced repellent called Lee's Sports Balm, which has a 14 percent concentration in a camphor-scented synthetic beeswax base. In fact, I rather prefer Sports Balm. It's even more resistant to washing than Cutter's, a useful feature if you sweat a lot or fish for trout.

My technique is to use Sports Balm or Cutter's on the exposed areas of my hide, and spray my legs, pants cuffs and sock tops with a spray repellent, usually Cutter's. A spray doesn't pack the wallop of a cream. It has a lower concentration of active ingredients, because it can't be directed as accurately. Deet has a way of chewing up certain plastics and some synthetic fabrics. It likes watch crystals, glasses, rayon, Dynel, and certain stretch materials like spandex. In other words, don't spray your girdle. It can irritate mucous membranes, and smarts like hell if you get it in your eyes. The spray's lower concentration and alcohol base, however, aren't as significant when applied to clothing, which doesn't sweat at all, or shins, which sweat very little. The spray's worth its weight.

But you can't get every inch of skin, though. Even Achilles had his heel. Most of the time, the best and most constructive approach to insect bites is to ignore them. If you're one of those poor souls — and most of my family is — who swell and itch for hours, I can recommend a paste make-up of Adolph's Meat Tenderizer and water. Somehow it digests a good bit of the toxins in an insect bite. Lacking this, a hard 30-second push on the bite with the eraser end of the pencil stub in your pack will disperse the toxins through a larger volume of your flesh, and they'll be less irritating.

For those of you who dislike chemicals with strange names, I offer a novel insect repellent technique that I learned from one of my *Habitant* kin years ago. Take a garlic bud and slice it up into little pieces. Swallow them whole and wait a while — say a couple of hours. Pop a fresh bud about every twelve hours, and the bugs shun you. Perhaps it alters the scent of your perspiration, but if it does, it's not noticeable. That's all right, the USDA doesn't really know why deet works, either.

BLISTERS

Let's talk first about prevention. Obviously, a well-fitted pair of boots, laced sufficiently firm to prevent them from rubbing, is a good beginning. Two pairs of socks is another help. Clean socks, free of dried sweat (for which read salt), can help, as can regular washing of the feet. Liberal applications of baby powder can help, too, and moleskin on your heels is just dandy, particularly on those first few hikes of the year when your feet are still tender. But sooner or later it'll happen.

Heel feels hot? Skin red? Act now, not later. An application of moleskin can stop the formation of a blister, but moleskin over an already-formed blister is a flaming horror, because when you peel off the moleskin, the rest of your skin comes off with it. Cut a doughnut of moleskin to fit around the blister. If the blister is open, cover it with an adhesive bandage over the moleskin and then apply a second doughnut over the bandage. I'm not a believer in antiseptics, preferring a good soap. Trak works well; so does Sutter's. A lot of people advocate popping the blister. I don't usually, since the blister will pop of its own accord. If it's a real big one, I'll pop it with a needle from the sewing kit that I've passed through the flame of a match. Scrub the area afterward.

ANKLES AND KNEES

If you're prone to lower joint problems — and even if you're not — the Ace bandage adds zilch weight and a lot of peace of mind.

Most injuries on the trail are minor. You can effectively cope with minor strains and sprains on the trail without using an ankle wrap, although it's a good idea to have one. So you've turned your ankle. Nothing serious. You can stand on it and can walk on it. But it hurts a little, and you'll be stiff in the morning. Keep your boots on at this time point, and move along slowly until you find a stream. Pick a comfortable rock, take off the boot, and immerse the foot and ankle in the stream. A good, long, relaxing soak. While you're doing this, parcel out some of the load in your pack to your companions. If everybody's pack is full, swap some heavy items for some lighter ones. If you have an Ace bandage, wrap the ankle. This will make you feel more secure and reduce any pain.

Start off again, at an easy pace. Don't push yourself too hard, and cut the trip short before your goal is reached, if need be. This is a good time to make early camp, soak the ankle again, and sprawl out on your polypad with your foot up on your pack while you stir the stew. The next day you'll probably be stiff but able to move with some security. In the unlikely event of a bad sprain, get back to civilization immediately after the soak and wrap treatment, because you'll probably move with considerable discomfort the next day.

SPECIAL NEEDS

I've said this before but feel compelled to say it again. If you have special medical requirements that necessitate the use of a prescription drug, don't go off into the outback without it. Asthma, diabetes, thyroid deficiency, angina — whatever — these conditions and many more require that you have relief or maintenance medication with you at all times.

On a simpler level, your vision may be sufficiently poor that breaking your glasses may leave you virtually helpless. In this case, you'd be ill advised to go on a trip without an extra pair stashed securely in your pack. You may be one of those poor souls who require sun glasses even in the relatively dull light of an Eastern sun. If you do, consider them a prescription drug and make sure they're with you. Protect your weaknesses.

SUNBURN

Along with blisters, sunburn rates as the great joy killer for the outdoorsman. True, the Western backpacker moving along a series of open ridges on a sunny day at ten thousand feet is more exposed than the Easterner along his shady trail. And the canoeist or the snow climber is far more prone to devastating sunburn than even the high country walker. But we do get sunny days in the East. I remember one in particular. The top of Dix Mountain in the Adirondacks on a clear day. The view from the summit is one of the finest and the alpine gardens were in bloom. This hot day I lounged in shorts for about two hours on the summit. Later that night, I was scarcely distinguishable from a healthy lobster. I was well tanned, and am fairly dark skinned to boot. But I really got done to a turn. Since then, I've been a bit wiser about sun protection in exposed areas.

Molly's found that sunscreens containing menthyl salicylate or oxybenzone work well, and sunscreens with a high percentage of para-animo benzoic acid work superbly. She's pretty much cozied up to a product called Class Five, a fairly expensive solution in an alcohol base available in most climbing shops. I find that an alcohol base lotion is too drying, so I prefer Glacier Creme, an English preparation available at your outfitters, or Sea and Ski.

The old rule of early exposure to the sun for short periods of time is a good one. It enables your skin to develop some protective pigmentation. Don't use a sunscreen for these fifteen minute bouts, as you'll be defeating your purpose. But please carry your sunscreen with you, and use it when you anticipate severe exposure. Watch out for hazy days. They can lull you into a false sense of security.

There's a simple treatment for most sunburn — cool water. If you're badly burned, you need medical attention.

DEHYDRATION

The fluid balance of the human body is delicate, but surprisingly flexible. On a hot day, a hardworking hiker may shed literally quarts of fluid in the form of sweat to cool the machinery. This fluid, and the salts contained in it, have to be replaced. The symptoms are reasonably dramatic. Dizziness, mild nausea, fatigue and muscle cramps are the commonest. The solution, fortunately, is simple. Relax, rehydrate your parched system with water, and replenish your salt supply with one or two salt tablets. Within five minutes you're feeling fine. Salt tablets are commonly available at drugstores without prescription. The commonest are Thermotabs or Thermodex. Molly and I both use salt tabs when we hike in warm weather, and we use Gatorade as well, usually just at lunch break and when we first hit camp.

HEAT EXHAUSTION

Heat exhaustion is a spectacular and alarming condition which is self-limiting but not necessarily serious. This is brought on as a result of long, hard work in a warm environment, and is caused by the dilation of blood vessels close to the skin so that they can carry off more heat. The effect is simply to reduce the blood supply to your brain, which causes you to feel dizzy and sick to the stomach. Your heartbeat becomes very rapid and irregular, and your skin feels clammy. Your body temperature isn't elevated. In fact, it may even be a bit lower than normal.

Lie down, preferably with your head slightly lower than the rest of your body, and sit up only to take fluids. In a few minutes you'll feel better. Now's the time to take a good breather, replenish your fluid supply, eat a little, and let the machinery return to normal. When you resume, take it easy.

HEAT STROKE

The fancy name for this is hyperpyrexia – a very dangerous condition that calls for prompt action. It occurs under the same circumstances as heat exhaustion, but the failure mode is different. Whereas heat exhaustion takes place while your body is cooling itself efficiently, almost too efficiently, heat stroke occurs when your cooling mechanism simply fails and your body can no longer cool itself by natural means. Typically, the victim complains of feeling unbearably hot, almost feverish; he stops perspiring and his body temperature climbs to dangerous levels. Disorientation and lack of coordination are symptoms; in a severe attack, the victim will pass out.

This condition is not self-limiting. It will grow worse if unattended, and in time the victim will either die or suffer irreversible physiological damage. Cool the victim's body as quickly as possible! The most effective way is to immerse him completely in water until his body temperature drops to less dangerous levels and he's rational again. If there isn't a lake or stream close by, soak his clothing with water from your canteens and fan him while somebody else goes off to refill the water supply.

Massage of the arms and legs promotes circulation in the extremities and helps cool the victim. Once the body temperature has been lowered and the victim is out of immediate danger, plans should be made to evacuate him. He may be able to travel for short distances without a pack, if he's cooled off frequently on the way, but heat stroke victims may lose a degree of control over their heat regulatory mechanism for some time and may be intolerant of heat for months afterward. Accordingly, evacuate the victim by stretcher or improvised litter if possible – even if he appears to be functioning fairly well.

Heat stroke happens most frequently to people who aren't wearing hats. If you're out in the sun for long periods of time doing heavy work, wear a hat. Cool your head and your whole body if you can in a friendly local stream. Maintain an adequate intake of fluids. And don't ignore heat stroke. It won't go away.

HYPOTHERMIA

We mentioned hypothermia earlier, but this is a good time to remind you again about this most unpleasant phenomenon. It's related in a way to heat stroke. With heat stroke, the body has lost its ability to cool itself. With hypothermia, the body has essentially lost its ability to generate enough heat to maintain normal core temperature. This means that no amount of insulation **by itself** can reverse hypothermia. This is important enough to repeat. No amount of insulation can aid a hypothermia victim, because he is unable to produce enough heat to warm his body to normal temperatures.

The victim must be stripped of all wet clothing to avoid further heat loss, and popped into a prewarmed sleeping bag. It may be necessary for another person to crawl in with him to provide an external source of heat. The victim should be immediately fed something warm. Soup, tea, coffee, it doesn't really matter. Soup or cocoa are probably the best choices, followed by carbohydrate-rich foods. This is also a time when the rules against fire building can be thrown out the window.

Build a fire, and keep that person warm. A space blanket (the fragile, aluminized, tensilized Mylar film kind) can serve as a very efficient reflector to direct the heat of the fire to the victim. Remember, he's in a nylon-shelled sleeping bag, and direct flame dotes on nylon and goose down.

It takes time for the body to recoup its losses. A severely chilled person may require as much as eight hours of warming, feeding, and more or less constant attention before he's ready to travel again. A particularly severe case, which can result in pulmonary edema, is very unlikely in an Eastern summer, but given the right combination of conditions, is possible. This is nothing to play games with. Prompt evacuation is required along with professional attention. Rewarming operations must be carried on vigorously and constantly.

14. NIGHT WALKIN'

"Shine it on, Harreye."
— R & R

Some time you'll find yourself walking in the woods at night, either by design or by accident. Most commonly, your first experience is by accident. It was a fine day and you found a deep, sheltered pool to skinnydip in, and all your plans for a six o'clock arrival at the trailhead were shot to hell by a little good old-fashioned hedonism. This is as it should be. Schedules are for the workadaddy world, not for backpacking. So now it's eight o'clock, twilight's crashing down around your ears, and you're four miles from your car.

Aarrgh! Panic! Take it easy. You're equipped to stay overnight, aren't you? You won't melt; you won't freeze; you won't starve. Sure, you may be late for work tomorrow, but that's not exactly the worst fate that could befall you. You're in no danger. With that in mind, simply start walking, with an easy, relaxed mind. You're about to learn something that will extend the boundaries of your pleasure.

The twilight will deepen almost imperceptibly, but you'll still be able to see, so don't panic and reach for a flashlight. If the trail's relatively free of steep, scrambly descents, and you can achieve a sufficiently calm head to let your body take over and do your walking for you, you'll find yourself out of the woods in two hours without once resorting to artificial light. Really. Your eyes grow accustomed to the deepening gloom, and your body makes a series of subtle, minute adjustments to realign its balance. If worst comes to worst, you still have your flashlight to get you through the rough spots in fine shape, although it will louse up your night vision if you use it too much.

As you get more and more involved with backpacking, you'll find that night walking is a great way to get into the boonies on a Friday night, avoiding the Saturday morning scramble and gaining another night in your friendly sleeping bag. If you're not far from home, you can get up at four o'clock on a Monday morning, walk quietly out in the magical mists of predawn, drive home, and still get to work on time.

Needless to say, if you're into night walking, you should carry an adequate light source. Not every trail lends itself to the old owl eyes routing. For ordinary trekking where you might require an occasional light around camp, a small AA cell flashlight is the best choice. The most popular is the little Mallory, and for good reason. It's very light, compact, fairly reliable, and produces a usable quantity of light. The AA-sized alkaline cells are remarkably long-lived. An excellent burrow-through-the-pack light.

For general camp illumination, I prefer the darkness modified by a small candle lantern. There are several choices: the classic folding lantern with mica (more likely plastic) windows, the telescoping French-made lantern designed to hang inside a tent, and a tiny cylindrical lantern using a flat candle called the Alpine. I'm scared of open flame inside a tent, but either the French lantern or the Alpine will work safely. The big folding jobbie is a fragile, rickety horror, although it throws the most light. I suggest the Alpine as the best compromise. No, it's not as efficient as a flashlight, but somehow friendlier, if you know what I mean.

The little Mallory flash is acceptable in a pinch for night walking, but no flashlight really throws a beam that's wide enough and soft enough for good, relaxed walking. A headlamp is a good compromise for night walking. A strap that encircles your head like a hatband without a hat holds it in place, and the battery pack clips onto your belt, leaving your hands free. There are several lightweight units around, the Pifco and the Wonder, and while they're all right, I won't call them rugged. *The* headlamp is a heavy, robust job made by Justrite. It uses four D cells, and comes with a frosted diffusing lens. You can also get low-drain bulbs for it. They're not as bright as the standard bulb, but they increase battery life greatly.

The advantages of the headlamp are obvious. Your hands are free to walk or to rummage, and the weight of the unit rides on your belt. The diffused beam is soft and wide, which makes for pleasant walking. The big (and heavy) battery pack is very dependable, and the unit functions well when wet.

My own preference is a carbide lamp for a longish night walk. Justrite, who made the lamp I'm using, has stopped building their classic brass lamps. They now build a plastic hideosity that's received some dreadful reports from cavers, although I suspect it would work for hikers. The best lamp available today is the English-made Premier, an old-timey brass lamp whose parts are generally interchangeable with the Justrite.

The carbide lamp is a fussy, eminently tinkerable, low cost source of vast amounts of bright light. Acetylene gas is burned by dripping water on calcium carbide, and it can be a small bomb if you don't have your head buttoned on straight. Further, storage of carbide is a hassle, because it must be kept dry, and disposal of a spent charge (a gray powder) should be done at home if possible because there are arsenic salts in the residue.

There's a lot of fuss and flummery about a carbide lamp. You need a few extra pieces of gear with them, for one. I carry a 100 cc polybottle of calcium carbide and an extra charging jar with a cap on it, filled and ready to go. I also carry a small polybottle containing a spare jewel tip, a flame protector that fits over the jewel tip to shield the flame on windy nights, a cleaning needle for the tip (VERY important), a spare gasket for the charging jar, and a spare felt. The felt diffuses the acetylene generated in the jar and scrubs it. If the felt is cruddy, the lamp is very unhappy. In a pinch, you can wash the felt, but it's easier to carry a spare. This bother will bring you the steady, bright, soft light of a well-tuned carbide lamp which is a joy to walk by, and makes setting up camp for four a breeze. You'll probably be better off with the big Justrite headlamp, but you can develop a genuine affection for a carbide lamp.

Assuming you'll try a carbide lamp, here's a little troubleshooting chart for the Premier and the old brass Justrite:

TROUBLE	CAUSE	REMEDY
No gas generated	No carbide in charging jar	Fill with carbide
No gas generated	No water in tank	Fill with water
No gas generated	Valve stuck — no water dripping into jar	Remove top, open water door and valve, blow through water door until flow starts. Doesn't work? Blow through stem.
Gas leak and/or flame around charging jar gasket	Worn gasket or untightened jar	Blow out flame and tighten jar. Replace gasket if it still leaks.
Popping and sputtering around jewel tip	Loose jewel tip	Blow out lamp and wait until it cools. Resecure jewel tip.
Lopsided flame	Worn jewel tip orifice	Replace jewel tip
Low flame or no flame when gas is being generated	Fouled jewel tip	Clean tip with needle
Little or no gas passing through tip when everything else is okay	Fouled felt	Replace felt, or wash in stream if you don't have a spare
Weakening flame	Charge is nearly spent, and the residue in the jar is absorbing the water	Increase water flow by turning valve to the right

Now that you have the lights you need, use them sparingly. It doesn't hurt at all, in this pushbutton world, to become, as Robert Frost captured it, "acquainted with the night." That small and unremembered trill of terror cutting through us is perhaps something we need to feel, however dimly in a world that's still only one flicker from the cave, and the glowing coals, and the unblinking eyes ringed around, waiting.

TRAILS END

". . . and so there ain't nothing more to write about, and I am rotten glad of it, because if I'd a knowed what a trouble it was to make a book I wouldn't a tackled it and aint't agoing to no more. But I reckon I got to light out for the Territory ahead of the rest, because Aunt Sally she's going to adopt me and sivilize me and I can't stand it. I been there before."

(THE ADVENTURES OF HUCKLEBERRY FINN, Mark Twain — New York: Charles L. Webster & Co. 1885)

And when you light out for the territories, may you travel always in the undiscovered country of your soul and the close, familiar country of your heart. And may you carry the swift lightness of your passage with you all your days.

H.N.R.
Rotterdam Junction, N.Y.